BEYOND THE NORM

A Salute to Missouri's
Norm Stewart

Columbia
Daily **Tribune**

SPORTS PUBLISHING INC.
www.SportsPublishingInc.com

Photo Editor: Mike Stewart
Coordinating Editor: Kent Heitholt
Director of Production: Susan M. McKinney
Interior and cover design: Terry N. Hayden
Book Layout: Susan M. McKinney and Jennifer A. Polson

In addition to the photo credits listed throughout the book, we wish to acknowledge credit for the following photos: page i , L.G. Patterson, *Columbia Daily Tribune*; page ii, University of Missouri Sports Information; page iv, Sean Meyers, *Columbia Daily Tribune*; page v, Lisa D. Finger, *Columbia Daily Tribune*; page 1, (clockwise) University of Missouri Sports Information; Lisa D. Finger, *Columbia Daily Tribune*; Denise McGill, *Columbia Daily Tribune*. Front cover photo by Brian W. Kratzer, *Columbia Daily Tribune*. Back cover photo courtesy of University of Missouri Sports Information.

ISBN: 1-58261-133-5
Library of Congress Number: 99-62922

Printed in the United States.

SPORTS PUBLISHING INC.
www.SportsPublishingInc.com

ACKNOWLEDGMENTS

When Norm Stewart announced his retirement on April 1, 1999, memories from his 36 years of playing and coaching Missouri Tiger basketball filled the hearts and thoughts of all Missouri fans. Taking over a team with a miserable losing record, Coach Stewart quickly turned the basketball program around and led the Missouri Tigers to national prominence. In his 32 years as coach, Stewart's Tigers won at least 20 games in 17 seasons, played in the NCAA Tournament 16 times and the NIT five times. To put all of this in proper perspective, the Missouri basketball program had only one postseason appearance (1944) before Coach Stewart's arrival.

During Coach Stewart's 36 years as a player and coach for the University of Missouri, the *Columbia Daily Tribune* gave its readers a front-row seat for every shot, every pass, and for every one of Stewart's 634 coaching victories at Missouri. His career total of 731 victories places Stewart seventh on the list of all-time winning coaches. But, as every Missouri fan knows, there is much more to Coach Stewart than the game on the court. His personal battle against cancer, his heroic efforts in founding Coaches vs. Cancer and his love for his family have all been subjects of poignant reporting in the *Tribune*.

Bringing Coach Stewart's amazing career to the pages of the *Tribune* required the hard work and dedication of many reporters, columnists, editors, executives and photographers at the paper. When we first approached the *Tribune* about this project, we received the enthusiastic support of Associate Publisher Vicki Russell and Managing Editor Jim Robertson. Once under way, the tireless efforts of Photo Editor Mike Stewart and Sports Editor Kent Heitholt made this book possible. Space limitations preclude us from thanking each writer and photographer whose work appears in the book. However, wherever available, we have preserved the writers' bylines and the photographers' credits to ensure proper attribution for their work.

At Sports Publishing Inc., we are grateful for the support of Susan McKinney, Jennifer Polson, Terry Hayden, Julie Denzer, Scot Muncaster, Joanna Wright, Terrence Miltner and Bret Kroencke.

Joseph J. Bannon, Jr.
Victoria J. Parrillo
Sports Publishing Inc.

TABLE OF CONTENTS

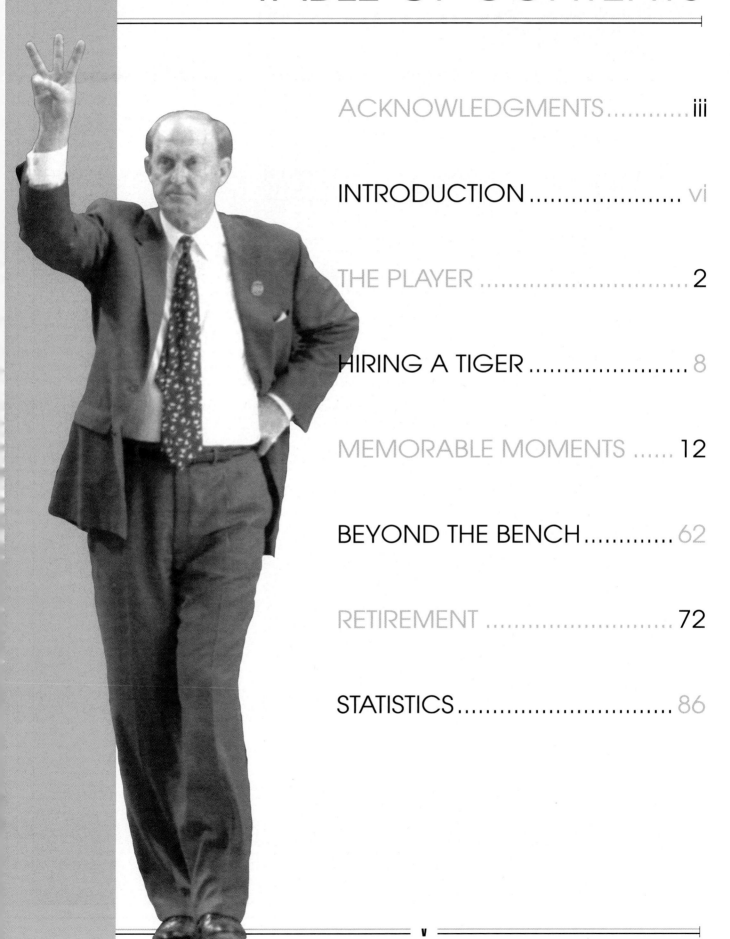

Introduction

• • • • • • • • • • • • •

He has memories: 36 points against Colorado and 33 against Iowa State in successive 1956 games, named MU head coach in 1967, Willie Smith's 43 points against Michigan in 1976, beating the mythical Irish in overtime at South Bend in 1980, victory over national powerhouse Louisville in 1982 ("Missouri is for real," they said), four straight conference titles by 1983, surviving cancer in 1989.

Then came 1994. Norm's Tigers were undefeated in the Big Eight, he was the AP Coach of the Year, he received the "Courage Award" by the American Cancer Society from President Bill Clinton and he was given the Outstanding Citizen of the Year Award by the Columbia Chamber of Commerce.

Nobody can write about Stewart's 32-year coaching career at Missouri without leaving out much of the good stuff. He's among the winningest coaches in Division I history. He is a legend.

We here in the shadow of the MU Columns are unable to ponder our good fortune without thinking about Norm Stewart. While still in good stride he handed his program to the next generation. A transition often less tranquil elsewhere was handled gracefully here, and the credit must go to the retiring coach.

Any future success the MU basketball program enjoys will have Norm Stewart's fingerprints all over it. He ran a fast leg.

–Hank Waters, Publisher
Columbia Daily Tribune

• • • • • • • • • • • • •

CHAPTER 1

Beyond the NORM

MU BRACES FOR BIG SEVEN BATTLE

FEBRUARY 10, 1956
Columbia Daily Tribune Staff

THE PLAYER

The University of Missouri basketball team, still holding title aspirations despite its 3-3 record in Big Seven conference competition, braced itself today for tomorrow night's invasion by second-place Iowa State College, the league's Cinderella team.

The game may well produce one of the season's brightest scoring duels between Missouri's Norm Stewart, who is back in form again after a back injury sidelined him three weeks ago, and Iowa State's Gary Thompson, whose floor game became a cause celebre several weeks ago when his coach, Bill Strannigan, accused Big Seven coaches and officials of ganging up on Thompson after a Kansas-Iowa State game at Lawrence.

Strannigan later withdrew the charge, but that didn't take Thompson out of the spotlight.

> **Stewart's current average in conference play is 20.5 points per game, while Thompson's is 16.3.**

Stewart's current average in conference play is 20.5 points per game, while Thompson's is 16.3.

The brightest spot in the Missouri picture has been the development of a better balanced Missouri attack. Charite Denny, Tiger center, stepped up with a 23-point barrage against Kansas at Lawrence last Monday night, and Lionel Smith, Rodger Egelhart and Bill Ross are all beginning to hit in double figures most of the time.

Coach Wilbur Stalcup will stick to that starting combination for the Tigers, and Strannigan has indicated that he will use his regular five with Chuck Vogt and Charles Crawford at the forwards, Don Medsker at center and Andre Garrde working with Thompson at the guards.

The game will be vital for the Tigers. Their loss of three games in six starts puts them on the border-line. Despite the fact that the league race already is so jumbled that the winner of the title may finish with three or four losses, the Tigers, at this halfway point in the campaign, can't afford another defeat on their home floor.

There will be a game between the Missouri B team and the Tiger fresh-men before the MU- Iowa State clash, and it will afford the Missouri follow-ers their first opportunity to see their first Negro athlete scholarship winner in action. Al Abram, who recently enrolled at the university after being graduated from St. Louis Summer High, will play with the freshmen.

Showing off the picture-perfect form that made him the team's leading scorer, Norm Stewart, left, joins Lionel Smith at a Missouri basketball practice. (Photo courtesy of University of Missouri Sports Information)

Beyond the NORM

VENGEFUL TIGERS

FEBRUARY 20, 1956
Columbia Daily Tribune Staff

Coach Wilbur Stalcup had his four-times-beaten University of Missouri basketball team in Ames today, poised for an effort to wreak the same kind of vengeance on the Iowa State Cyclones tonight that it wreaked on the Colorado Buffaloes before a crowd of 4,800 in Brewer Field House last Saturday.

The Tigers bowed to Colorado at Boulder three weeks ago and uncorked terrific basket-shooting heat to slap down the Buffs 86-81, when Bebe Lee brought his charges here for their return visit.

Nine days ago the Bengals were beaten, 85-88, by Iowa State in a Brewer Field House overtime game. It's for that thumping the Bengals are seeking vengeance at Ames tonight—vengeance and a continued hold on a tiny thread of hope that they may yet stage a comeback and win the title after four early season conference defeats.

The Iowans beat Nebraska, a team which beat Missouri at Lincoln Saturday night, to move into a tie

In addition to starring on the Tigers' basketball team, Stewart also took the mound for the Missouri baseball squad. Here, he is shown pitching in 1954 for the Tiger team that won the NCAA Championship. (Photo courtesy of University of Missouri Sports Information)

with Kansas State for first place in the Big Seven race.

The Missouri victory over the title-defending Buffaloes Saturday night was decisive. The Tigers moved out in front early in the contest, and set a terrific pace all the way. Leading the blistering attack was Norm Stewart, whose 36 points were a new record for an individual shooter in the field house and carried him beyond the 1,000-point mark for his varsity career. Stewart scored 10 points in the first half, hitting 8 for 16 from the field for 50 percent in the first half. But even that hot pace was below the team average. The Bengals collected on an almost unbelievable 52.9 percent of their shots from the field before the intermission. They didn't slow up much afterward, for their average for the game was 46.1 against 33.3 for Colorado.

The Bengals weren't only hot from the floor—particularly on Stewart's and Lionel Smith's outside shots—but they played superbly on the boards as they dented Colorado's hopes of retaining the conference title.

Coach Wilbur Stalcup, as he set out for Ames yesterday afternoon, said he will keep intact the starting lineup he has been using ever since he promoted Rodger Egelhoff to a starting role. With Egelhoff will be Bill Ross at forward, Charles Denny at center and Stewart and Smith at guards.

Others making the trip with Stalcup, Assistant Coach Gerald Hedgepeth and Trainer Fred Wappel are Paul Stehr, Jon Paden, John Stephens, Jim Cotter, Redford Reichert, Truman Blacman and Eddie Ronsick.

While the Tigers were heading north by bus yesterday, Coach Bebe Lee, winding up his chores as basketball coach for the Buffs before he became director of athletics at Kansas State, put his charges aboard a plane for Norman, where Colorado meets Oklahoma tonight.

Norm Stewart (22) goes after a rebound in the Tigers' 1955 battle against Kansas. (Photo courtesy of University of Missouri Sports Information)

Beyond the NORM

STEWART HITS 33

FEBRUARY 21, 1956
Columbia Daily Tribune Staff

With Norman Stewart hitting 33 points, the University of Missouri knocked Iowa State out of a tie for leadership in the Big Seven basketball championship race last night at Ames and returned home today to begin preparations for the home game with Oklahoma here Saturday night.

The final score was 73 to 66.

The Cyclone loss, coupled with Kansas State's 73-50 victory over Nebraska last night, left Kansas State alone in the lead with a 7-2 record. The Tigers, with a mathematical chance to overtake the leaders, have a 5-4 record in the conference, while Iowa State is second with 6-3 and Colorado, which defeated Oklahoma 61-53 last night, is third with 5-3, Kansas fifth with 4-4, Nebraska sixth with 2-6 and Oklahoma last with 1-8.

Missouri led from early in the first half in avenging an 88-85 overtime loss to the Cyclones 10 days ago at Columbia.

Stewart split his night's production almost evenly, scoring 16 points in the first half and 17 in the final period. Early in the first half he hit five straight from the field as the Tigers gained leads of 10 and 12 points. Missouri led at the half 33-23.

> Stewart split his night's production almost evenly, scoring 16 points in the first half and 17 in the final period.

Iowa State made its only serious threat late in the final period, climbing to within one point at 52-51 and 54-53 before Missouri moved away.

Missouri hit 46 percent of its shots from the field while Iowa State managed only 35. John Crawford led Cyclone scorers with 21 points, 15 of them on free throws.

Kansas State's Wildcats wrapped up their seventh conference victory over Nebraska, while Colorado handed Oklahoma its eighth league defeat in nine games.

Each team plays a 12-game league schedule, so mathematically Iowa State, Colorado, Missouri and Kansas are still in the race. Iowa State can keep alive its hopes and the hopes of the other contenders by dumping K-State in one of three league games Saturday night.

However, the Cyclones have to do it on K-State's home court at Manhattan.

Kansas and Missouri should have an easier time.

The Jayhawks play Nebraska at Lincoln while Missouri meets Oklahoma at Columbia. Colorado is idle until next Monday when Iowa State goes to Boulder.

Nebraska stayed in the game with K-State until the second half.

Fritz Schneider scored six straight points as the last period opened to give the Wildcats a 41-34 lead. K-State coasted home from there.

Oklahoma bowed despite center Leroy Bacher's 30-point scoring spree.

Practice makes perfect. During the Tigers' 1956 season, Stewart set a fieldhouse record with 36 points against Colorado. In the same game, he also passed the 1,000 point total for his career. (Photo courtesy of University of Missouri Sports Information)

CHAPTER 2

Beyond the NORM

STEWART IS NEW TIGER COACH

MARCH 10, 1967
Columbia Daily Tribune Staff

N orman Stewart, former University of Missouri basketball and baseball star, has been named head basketball coach at the University to succeed Bob Vanatta, who has resigned, Chancellor John Schwada announced this afternoon.

Stewart, head basketball coach at the State College of Iowa for the past six years, will assume his duties here next Wednesday. He was formerly freshman coach at the university in basketball and baseball after his graduation in 1956.

Stewart's appointment was approved today by the University Board of Curators.

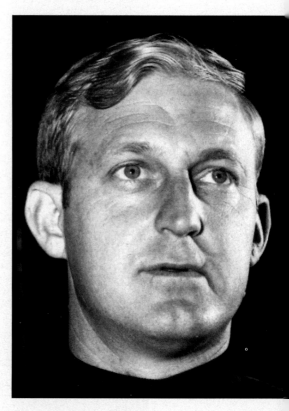

Norm Stewart takes charge of the Missouri basketball program. (Photo courtesy of University of Missouri Sports Information)

HIRING A TIGER

Norm Stewart and his wife, Virginia, enjoy the Christmas season.
(Photo courtesy of University of Missouri Sports Information)

Beyond the NORM

STEWART GETS FAST START

MARCH 12 ,1967
Charlie Paulsell

Norman Stewart, Missouri's new head basketball coach, is wasting no time in getting on the recruiting trail.

Shortly after the announcement Friday afternoon of his appointment as successor to Bob Vanatta, the 32-year-old former Tiger basketball and baseball standout boarded a plane at Cedar Falls, Iowa, where he has been head coach at the State College of Iowa for six years, and flew to St. Louis to scout the semifinals and finals of the State Class L Tournament there.

He was joined in St. Louis by Bob Price, MU freshman coach, and early Saturday morning the two drove to Highland, Illinois, to visit a prospect they hope to recruit, then returned to St. Louis for the Saturday night session of the state tourney.

Stewart, who described himself as "thrilled" by his appointment to the head job at his alma mater, planned to spend a few hours in Columbia this afternoon, then return to Cedar Falls to wind up his affairs there and be back on the job by Wednesday or Thursday.

"It's a thrill and it's very satisfying to me that the university has given me this responsibility and I'm eager to get started," Stewart told the *Tribune* in a telephone interview from St. Louis Saturday.

> "It's a thrill and it's very satisfying to me that the university has given me this responsibility and I'm eager to get started," Stewart told the Tribune.

"I realize it's going to be a tough job and that it's going to take some positive thinking but I think we can get somewhere when we can get organized and keep things moving in the right direction. I hope that the coaches in the state and the alumni will continue to give me their support.

"In talking with some of the high school coaches and other people, I've learned that the state has had a good year talent-wise. I hope we can convince some of these boys that the University of Missouri is a great institution and a good place for them to play their college basketball.

"Bob Price has been very helpful in going over what has been done in the way of recruiting efforts thus far and the contacts which have been made. The first day for signing basketball letters of intent is April 4 and that's only a little more than three weeks away so time is a very important factor."

At the State College of Iowa, Stewart produced conference championship teams in 1962 and 1964 and his overall record for his six seasons there was 97 victories and 42 defeats. His tenure at the Iowa school followed four years as freshman basketball and baseball coach at Missouri, where he won all-conference honors in basketball and pitched a baseball no-hitter before finishing his eligibility in 1956. He later played both professional baseball and basketball before joining the MU staff as an aide to then head coach Sparky Stalcup.

Stewart's appointment last week was recommended by Athletic Director Don Faurot and Dan Devine, head football coach, who will assume the athletic directorship upon Faurot's retirement June 30. It was approved unanimously by the Committee on Intercollegiate Athletics and later by the Board of Curators.

Stewart said that his wife, the former Virginia Zimmerly of Kansas City, and their three children probably will not join him here until after school closes in Cedar Falls in June.

"We built a home in Cedar Falls and moved into it only last December," Stewart said. "Of course, we'll put it on the market now and if a buyer wants immediate possession, we'll let him have it. Otherwise, the family will stay there until school is out."

The Stewart children are Jeffrey, 9; Scott, 6; and Laura, 3.

Coach Stewart's relentless recruiting during the early years of his career at Missouri laid the groundwork for the national prominence that his teams would achieve over the next three decades. (Photo courtesy of University of Missouri Sports Information)

CHAPTER 3

Beyond the NORM

MEMORABLE MOMENTS

MU'S SMITH MAKES FINAL GAME MEMORABLE

MARCH 21, 1976
Greg Haney

LOUISVILLE—What more can be said of Willie Smith? What words can aptly describe such artistry in the game of basketball?

What string of nouns, adjectives and verbs is adequate to portray his twisting jump shot or his ability to defy a defense?

There are none. Only the act is left to describe itself. And those who try to relate what they've seen. So it was yesterday at Freedom Hall when Missouri's Smith, a left-hander with a right way of doing things, scored 43 points in the Tigers' 95-88 loss to Michigan (24-6) in the National Collegiate Athletic Association's Midwest regional final.

It was senior Smith's final appearance in a Mizzou uniform. For Michigan, it is on to the NCAA semifinals in Philadelphia and a matchup with East regional winner Rutgers on Saturday.

Smith was given the regional's Most Valuable Player award for his 30-

and 43-point performances in two regional games. He would have much preferred the trophy which the Wolverines took home.

Smith's performance defies what most words on paper can convey. Listen, instead, to the observers for a clue to Smith's brilliance.

"Willie Smith put on one of the greatest shooting exhibitions that I have ever seen," Michigan coach Johnny Orr said. "And we had him covered pretty good too."

"That's the greatest thing I've ever seen," MU forward Kim Anderson said.

"He (Smith) is the Bob McAdoo of college basketball," Smith's roommate, James Clabon said.

"Willie Smith proved that if he's not the best, then I'd like to see him (who's better)," Missouri coach Norm

Before the game, Coach Stewart strikes a familiar pose on the Missouri bench. (Columbia Daily Tribune)

Coach Stewart shares a smile with DePaul's legendary Ray Meyer. (Columbia Daily Tribune)

Stewart remarked. "And I'm not going to take any credit for coaching him."

Smith's 43-point performance was the third highest total for a game by a Missouri player. He also took down seven rebounds and had three assists and two steals.

Joe Scott's 46 points against Nebraska in 1961 are the most points ever scored by a Tiger in a game.

During one seven-minute span in the second half, Smith hit for 15 points, mostly on long, floating jump shots from 20-25 feet out. He almost single-handedly brought MU from 63-52 deficit to a 76-71 lead with 7:54 remaining in the game.

His three-point play at the 7:54 mark, a 27-foot jumper on which Michigan's Rickey Green fouled him, put a cap on his spectacular shooting spree. It put the assemblage in Freedom Hall in wonderment.

But Smith's one-man stand couldn't overcome the balanced Michigan attack. The Wolverines put four men in double figures, with junior guard Rickey Green leading the way with 23 points.

Michigan withstood MU's comeback, gathered momentum at the four-minute mark and came on to capture the Midwest regional title.

"We got started wrong in the first half, made a tremendous comeback, had the game and missed the free throws," Stewart said. "I wish there had been a little less time when we got up."

The Tigers, normally a 72-

percent free-throwing team, hit 10 of 22 free throws. Crucial misses of one-and-one situations in the final 10 minutes undid Missouri's chances.

After Smith's 15-point spurt put Mizzou ahead, 76-71, with 7:54 to play, Michigan's Green scored twice and forward John Robinson added two free throws to tie the game at 77 with 6:14 to go.

Then Robinson, fouled by senior Mark Anderson, put Michigan ahead to stay, 79-78, with a pair of free

Stewart studies the Tigers' play during a preseason game in Columbia. (Columbia Daily Tribune)

throws. Freshman center Stan Ray, who scored 13 points and had 15 rebounds coming off the bench, got outmaneuvered under the boards shortly thereafter by Michigan freshman center Phil Hubbard on an inbounds play and the Wolverines had an 81-78 lead.

Mark Anderson brought MU back to within one, 81-80, with a 14-foot jumper with 4:04 to go. But that was Mizzou's last close moment. Two quick baskets by Robinson and forward Wayman Britt moved the lead to five, and Missouri never could catch up.

"If we had done a few different things, a few little things, it might have been different," Kennedy said. "Missing free throws happens every once in a while and it's a hard thing to explain. It's too bad it had to happen in this game."

"A few breaks and it could have gone either way," Smith said. "There are teams in the Big Eight as quick as Michigan."

Someone mentioned his 43-point accomplishment again. Was it any consolation for losing?

Stewart gets his point across with a little one-on-one discussion.
(Columbia Daily Tribune)

"It's not important," Smith said. "My mother saw the game on television and she'll be proud."

"He (Smith) played so well, and I feel so bad to see him lose," Kim Anderson added.

"We will miss him a little," Kennedy understated. "He's a heck of a nice guy and his true colors showed. What he did today tells you something about him."

"The way Willie was shooting," Kim Anderson said, "that (Smith shooting a lot) is the way it should be.

"It's a shame it's taken this long for Smith to get national recognition."

Perhaps someone closest to the action, a player, could describe, give a why and a how and a word as to what Smith does. Maybe a teammate knows how to express the secret.

"I can't think of any words to describe what he does," Kim Anderson concluded.

The experience goes down with the moment. Forty-three points. One thousand, three hundred and eighty-seven career points.

You'll never see Willie Smith play another game for the University of Missouri.

Coach Stewart's 1973 Tigers captured the Big 8 Pre-Season Basketball Tournament. (Columbia Daily Tribune)

MISSOURI DESTROYS IRISH MYTH

MARCH 9, 1980
Kirk Wessler

LINCOLN—Bedlam reigned. Phlogdo of the Ozone, one of those raucous members of the Antlers, stood on the NCAA logo pasted to one corner of the basketball floor at Devaney Sports Center and did a wild and crazy rendition of the St. Vitus' dance.

Missouri guard Larry Drew slapped hands with people he had never seen in his entire life. Black-and-gold-clad cheerleaders clung together in mob scenes of pure, uninhibited joy.

The myth had been destroyed. There are no halos in South Bend, Indiana.

Missouri beat Notre Dame 87-84 in overtime yesterday to earn a berth in the semifinals of the Midwest regional next Friday night in Houston. The Tigers' opponent will be the winner of today's second-round game between Louisiana State and Alcorn State. But there will be plenty of time for planning tomorrow. Maybe by then the smiles will have faded from the faces of the Missouri players—at least a little bit.

Then again, maybe not.

It is nearly impossible to describe the electricity Missouri generated here yesterday. Playing before a national television audience and a deafening crowd of 14,558, the Tigers beat the Irish, the national team,

> "I guess I don't even realize it yet, how big a game this was to the University of Missouri," said Tiger forward Mark Dressler.

and Coach Digger Phelps. They did it with only nine players—all that's left of a once deep and multitalented team.

Most of all, they did it by playing 45 minutes of the hardest, most intense basketball you'll ever see.

And by the end, they had the crowd—all but a tiny section of Notre Dame faithful—cheering their every move.

"I guess I don't even realize it yet, how big a game this was to the University of Missouri," said Tiger forward Mark Dressler, who scored 32 points and played the game of his young life. "I just don't realize what we've done."

Everybody who watched this game knows what Dressler did.

The 19-year-old sophomore, who stepped into the starting lineup only 2 1/2 weeks ago when Curtis Berry went down with a knee injury, made 13 of 16 shots, six of eight free throws, pulled down eight

Hard work, dedication and attention to detail both during the game and in practice were key ingredients in Coach Stewart's 731 career victories, 634 of which came at the University of Missouri. (Columbia Daily Tribune)

rebounds and eventually made the steal that clinched the victory.

But Dressler had plenty of help. Drew, the lone senior starter and the team captain, scored 15 points and dished out a school-record 12 assists. Center Steve Stipanovich, who chose Missouri over Notre Dame last spring after a highly publicized recruiting war, scored 15 points and had eight rebounds. Forward Ricky Frazier added 14 points and freshman guard Jon Sundvold, playing with poise far beyond his 18 years, added 10 points and did not commit a single turnover.

Never, not even for a second of this tension-packed contest, did Missouri seem awed by the Irish or their pull-it-out-with-a-miracle tradition.

"Coach Stewart told us before the game," said Stipanovich. "He said we've got to realize they don't walk around with halos over their heads."

For a while, however, it seemed as though Notre Dame might prove Missouri Coach Norm Stewart a liar.

Missouri, which had trailed by six points at halftime, took a 76-74 lead when Stipanovich took a pass from Sundvold and got behind Irish center Orlando Woolridge for a layup with 35 seconds left in regulation.

Using his own competitive fire and sideline intensity to motivate his ballclub was always one of Coach Stewart's greatest strengths. (Columbia Daily Tribune)

When Notre Dame tried to work the ball inside at the other end, Stipanovich deflected a pass into the corner. Drew picked it up, but Woolridge grabbed the ball, too. The two players went down in a heap and a jump ball was called. Trash, coins and boos showered the floor as 14,000 people protested that a foul should have been called on Woolridge.

"It was a good call," said Drew. "He had a hold of the ball, and I kind of slung my body into his. And he still had a hold of the ball. Good call."

Woolridge won the tip, then floated underneath the basket, took a long pass from Kelly Tripucka and tied the score on a layup with four seconds left.

Missouri called for time out, but the clock ran down to one second before stopping. Stewart, who had been called for a technical foul in the first half, was livid, especially when game officials refused to put any time back on the clock.

"We could have won it in regulation," Stewart said. "We should have. But they just seemed unwilling to put time back on the clock . . . after deep consultation."

So when Missouri's inbounds pass was batted away, the game headed for overtime.

Tripucka, who scored 22 points and kept the Irish alive throughout with deadly outside shooting, fouled out 22 seconds into the extra period, and Missouri was off to a good start. The Tigers took the lead, 78-76, on a pair of free throws by Drew, but the Irish tied the

Norm Stewart and assistant coach Kim Anderson watch the action at the Hearnes Center. (Sean Meyers, Columbia Daily Tribune)

game twice on field goals by Tracy Jackson, who finished with a team-high 27 points.

But with MU on top, 82-80 in the final 30 seconds of play, Notre Dame's Bill Hanzlik missed a 10-footer in the lane. Dressler rebounded and was fouled by Jackson. His two free throws gave Missouri an 84-80 lead, and the game was never tied again.

Dressler put Notre Dame away for good when he dived to steal the dribble from Woolridge with seven seconds left. A foul by Irish guard John Paxson sent Dressler to the line again, and he sank two more free throws to give Missouri an 87-82 lead.

"I had a pretty good idea who was going to win right then," said Stipanovich. "It required a miracle for Notre Dame to win."

Coach Stewart and the Missouri bench await the result of a three-point shot. (Jim Noelker, Columbia Daily Tribune)

This time, the Irish didn't get one.

"I would like to congratulate the University of Missouri," said Phelps, whose team finished the season 22-6. "I thought they were just unbelievably disciplined. They had to have shot at least 70 percent in the second half, and that to me is unbelievable basketball. They played a great game."

Actually, the Tigers shot only 68 percent in the second half, but that was good enough to give them a 60.7 percent performance for the game—the 12th time this season they have been over the 60 percent mark. In fact, the Tigers shot almost as well from the field as Notre Dame shot from the free-throw line (61.5 percent).

Stewart apparently pulled out all the stops to get his team ready for this game.

"He really wanted to win," Stipanovich said. "I think even more so than the players did."

Before the game, Stewart had been presented a gold boutonniere by former graduate assistant Mike Aslin. "Here," Aslin said, pinning the flower on Stewart's lapel. "You've got to have this for Digger."

Phelps, who almost always sports a green carnation in his lapel for big games, didn't have one yesterday.

Futhermore, Curtis Berry, one of the injured Tiger players, made a surprise appearance in the locker room just before the Tigers took the floor. Berry was released yesterday from Columbia Regional Hospital where he underwent knee surgery. He spent most of the game with his leg propped up on a chair, but stood behind the bench with the aid of crutches during the overtime.

"Good medicine," Stewart said.

Very good, indeed.

Coach Norm Stewart after
a Missouri game.
(Columbia Daily Tribune)

Beyond the NORM

MISSOURI IS FOR REAL

JANUARY 18, 1982
Kirk Wessler

ST. LOUIS—This one was for respect: Missouri 69, Louisville 55. And when it was all but over, NBC-TV commentator Al McGuire verbalized the verdict for those several million nationwide viewers who might have seen but still couldn't quite believe.

"This is for the rest of the country," McGuire said. "Gang, Missouri is for real."

To the skeptics, to those who had scoffed at the Tigers' undefeated record—"Yeah, but they haven't played anybody good; wait till they play Louisville"—and even to many of the 18,664 partisan fans in the Checkerdome yesterday, it came as a shock.

It shouldn't have. Nor, for that matter, should it have been necessary for the second-ranked Tigers to prove their validity as a national power. In the past 10 years under Coach Norm Stewart, they've already had six 20-victory seasons and, at 14-0 so far this year, are certainly headed for a seventh. They've been to the National Invitation Tournament twice, the old Commissioner's Tournament once and to the NCAA Tournament four times. Once, in 1976, they even came within a whisker of making the Final Four.

> "I think," Missouri center Steve Stipanovich said, "people are going to start respecting us. There'll be people now that say, 'Hey, Missouri has got a good ballclub.'"

Still, to Joe Fan in New York City, in Birmingham, in Peoria, in Corvallis or even down at Harpo's in Columbia, Louisville is synonymous with basketball excellence, and Missouri is not. Make that was not.

"I think," Missouri center Steve Stipanovich said, "people are going to start respecting us. There'll be people now that say, 'Hey, Missouri has got a good ballclub.'"

Notions to the contrary have simply gone the way of other myths:

•   First, the Tigers blitzed Illinois, overcoming the rap that they weren't quick.

•   Then, they won two tough games on the West Coast against good teams, Alabama-Birmingham and Southern Cal, largely without the services of their two most renowned players, Stipanovich and Ricky Frazier. That zapped the belief that MU was a one- or two-man show.

• Yesterday, the Tigers put to rest the misguided impression that they cannot run, or that they can be easily beaten in a transition game.

That thought had surfaced again Saturday, perpetrated over the regional television airwaves by Louisville's appropriately nicknamed Lancaster "Flash" Gordon. Missouri, Gordon had figured, couldn't run with Louisville.

"I saw that," Missouri guard Jon Sundvold said. "Right then, I knew they didn't realize how we play. We play better when teams run with us."

But there is one basic difference between the way these two teams run: Louisville runs dumb; Missouri runs smart. That, as much as anything, explains the outcome of yesterday's game.

"Louisville will give you a few baskets just to get you in transition," Stewart explained.

So he told the Tigers to make sure to take good shots, to not force the break when it wasn't there and to beat Louisville back on defense. With just a couple of exceptions, Missouri did its job well.

"Our plan," Missouri guard Prince Bridges said, "was to neutralize their fast break and get out on

ours."

Said Sundvold: "We wanted to put the break right back on top of them. But if we didn't get the layup, we'd just get the ball back out and set up. Louisville's different. They get behind and start running and taking those 25-footers. We pull it back out, and that's what makes us a little better ballclub."

Louisville (11-4) jumped to an 8-2 lead in the game,

Coach Norm Stewart and a Tiger fan. (Columbia Daily Tribune)

largely because Missouri came out a wee bit tight and slightly intimidated by the Cardinals' habit of playing above the rim. Stipanovich had a shot blocked and rushed another to avoid getting blocked again. Sundvold forced one, and Moon McCrary missed a jumper off the break.

But after the first five minutes, the Tigers settled down and began to peck away. At 6:34 of the first half, Frazier, who scored a game-high 22 points and whom NBC named as the game's outstanding player, sank two free throws to tie the score at 20. Twenty seconds later, Bridges hit a jumper from the top of the key, and Missouri had the lead, 22-20.

Louisville, which entered the game ranked 17th nationally, managed to stay close for a couple more minutes. But then Tiger reserve guard Michael Walker wrecked the Cardinals for good, scoring eight points in the final 4 1/2 minutes of the half—six of those in the last 46 seconds—as Missouri raced to a 38-24 halftime lead that left Louisville for dead and the crowd in hysterics.

"We started out tight," McCrary said, "but Michael came in and loosened us up."

Walker replaced Sundvold with 4:47 left in the half. The first time he got his hands on the ball, he wheeled into the lane and put up a one-handed jump shot that looked terribly ill-conceived—before it swished through the net.

With 90 seconds left in the half, the 6-foot-4, 230-pound junior from Kansas City started his splurge with an assist to McCrary. Then, in the final minute, Walker threw in another jump shot, scored a layup off a pass from Sundvold and stole a pass at halfcourt and drove for yet another jumper.

All last week, Stewart had downplayed this game as being relatively unimportant, and he wasn't about to change that stance after winning.

"I didn't think I would get out there and get the baskets I got," said Walker, who finished with 14 points on six-of-seven shooting and two free throws. "Louisville is quick, but a couple times, they lapsed on defense and I got the easy shots."

Louisville never really threatened in the second half. Although Missouri failed to score a field goal on its first seven possessions of the period, the Cardinals could come no closer than nine points the rest of the way.

McCrary, whose considerable defensive reputation is beginning to precede him wherever he goes, turned Louisville forward Derek Smith inside out, allowing the 6-6 Olympian only two field goals in eight tries and a total of seven points. For the Cardinals, only Gordon scored in double figures, hitting 14 points.

As expected, Louisville won the battle of the boards handily, 40-27. But it hardly mattered. When Missouri needed a critical rebound, Stipanovich grabbed it with authority, one time flattening 6-8, 215-pound Charles Jones in the process. The official statistics credited Stipo with seven rebounds—although it seemed he claimed twice that many.

Offensively, the Tigers shot a low 48.8 percent, mostly because Stipanovich hit only one of eight shots. But they displayed good balance, getting 12 points from Bridges and 11 from McCrary. Sundvold provided five assists. As a team, Missouri committed only 10 turnovers, while Louisville had 18.

In the end, Stewart said he was pleased with the effort—although he reiterated that he didn't think the game should have been scheduled for noon the day after a night conference game with Nebraska.

All last week, Stewart had downplayed this game as being relatively unimportant, and he wasn't about to change that stance after winning.

Not so, some of the players.

"This was a big game for the whole team," Walker said. "A lot of people around the country probably didn't think we could play against a big team, even though we're ranked No. 2. But I think this proves that Missouri means business."

Stewart shows off some of his Big Eight Conference championship trophies. (Photo courtesy of University of Missouri Sports Information)

PEELER GETS THE LAST WORD

JANUARY 21, 1990
Mike Holtzclaw

S ome people really get into the Missouri-Kansas rivalry. Anthony Peeler lives it. He's been living it since he was a small child growing up in Kansas City, the middle ground of the rivalry.

Therefore, he had a different perspective on the hoopla surrounding yesterday's showdown at the Hearnes Center than some of his teammates did.

"All these Detroit guys told me that there wasn't really a rivalry for them," Peeler said. "I was sitting there thinking, 'It's a big rivalry to me.' I didn't want to go home and have everybody on my case, talking about how they beat us. I wanted to go home with a lot of confidence and say that we beat the No. 1 team today."

On the court, Peeler made sure that he wouldn't go home hanging his head, scoring a game-high 24 points to lead No. 4 Missouri to a 95-87 victory over No. 1 Kansas.

Peeler played 39 minutes and did a little bit of everything. He offset a cold touch from the field with a 14-for-14 showing from the free-throw line. He pulled down nine rebounds, passed for seven assists and had three steals.

> "I wanted to go home with a lot of confidence and say that we beat the No. 1 team today."
>
> —Anthony Peeler

"Anthony Peeler is so athletic, he exposes your weaknesses in a lot of different ways," Kansas coach Roy Williams said. "I really think he is so talented, it's unbelievable."

If things had stacked up a little differently a few years ago, Peeler might have been wearing the Jayhawks' blue uniform yesterday.

When he was growing up, he always watched the Jayhawks more than the Tigers, mainly because of the proximity of the Lawrence campus. His heroes were Cedric Hunter and Archie Marshall.

But, in the early signing period before his senior season at Paseo High School, Peeler took a good look at the two teams and signed with Missouri. Never mind that Kansas was on its way to a national championship that year; he figured that Missouri was the team that had a better chance of rising to national prominence in the coming years.

Norm Stewart, center, is amused as he listens in on a conversation between Missouri's Jeff Warren and an official. (L.G. Patterson, Columbia Daily Tribune)

"I just put the teams together," Peeler said. "The Doug Smiths and Nathan Buntins and Lee Cowards were coming to Missouri. The big players were leaving at Kansas, and with Larry Brown, there were expectations of him leaving up in the air. That's why I came to Missouri."

Now Peeler is a big reason that the Tigers have risen to the top. Yesterday's victory, coupled with Connecticut's upset of No. 2 Georgetown, should land the Tigers in the top spot of the national polls.

Peeler's shooting from the field has been somewhat erratic this season, as the athletic sophomore has often fallen into a pattern of putting up off-balance shots or running jumpers. Yesterday, he was shooting freely from the field, often without setting his feet, and he finished the day with five field goals in 15 attempts.

"He's a sophomore, and at that age, the concentration isn't what it needs to be," Missouri coach Norm Stewart said. "But I don't worry too much about him. He'll play both ends of the court and play well."

And he'll hit some free throws. Peeler came into the game hitting 76 percent. On Tuesday, with nine seconds left in a tie game against Oklahoma State, his confidence at the line was shaken ever so briefly when the crowd distracted him into missing his first free throw. Then he quickly regained his composure and sank the game-winning shot in a 72-71 victory.

"I've been real confident at the line ever since I hit that last shot at Oklahoma State," Peeler said.

Yesterday, he hit his free throws—and came up with an answer for a lot of people in Kansas City.

"My friends were talking about how KU was going to beat us," Peeler said. "I'm going to have to talk to a lot of people when I go home. I'm going to be calling a lot of my friends and saying, 'Look what we did.'"

Stewart, left, and assistant Bob Sundvold, 1990, on the sidelines at the Hearnes Center. (Columbia Daily Tribune)

Two of Missouri's stars in the early 1990s were Doug Smith and Anthony Peeler. Smith (above) receives Coach Stewart's applause at the Hearnes Center. Peeler (left) was an AP second-team All-American in 1992. (Photos by Columbia Daily Tribune)

Coach Stewart talks about shooting skills with summer campers, grades 4-12, during his annual basketball camp. (Lisa D. Finger, Columbia Daily Tribune)

Norm Stewart sits in then-Missouri Governor John Ashcroft's chair in 1990. The team visited the Missouri Capitol after beating Kansas. (Columbia Daily Tribune)

Beyond the NORM

ILLINI STAY CAUGHT IN MU STREAK

DECEMBER 23, 1993
David Holzman

ST. LOUIS—Missouri came to the St. Louis Arena just wanting to play a complete game in its annual matchup with Illinois.

The Tigers might have settled for just a good first half. They got and gave much more than was bargained for.

In their farewell to the Arena, the Tigers produced multiple comebacks to beat the No. 19 Fighting Illini 108-107 in triple overtime.

"We've got the sick and wounded playing for us," Missouri coach Norm Stewart said. "I guess women and children were next."

Three of Missouri's starters including leading scorer Jevon Crudup and point guard Melvin Booker fouled out. Mark Atkins, without whose three-point touch Missouri wouldn't have made up a nine-point deficit in the last 1:20 of regulation, and reserves Julian Winfield and Marlo Finner also fouled out.

The Tigers (6-1) stayed in and eventually won with freshmen Jason Sutherland, Derek Grimm and Kelly Thames joining seniors Lamont Frazier and Reggie Smith, making his first appearance in three weeks, on the floor.

With the additional 15 minutes, the Tigers got at least the 40 good ones they've been searching for all season. Crudup led Missouri to by far its best first half of the season. He was eight of 11 from the field and scored 18 of his team-high 22 points in the first half. Aided by Marlo Finner's three-pointer in the final seconds, Missouri led 42-38 at halftime.

"We know how good Crudup is," Illinois coach Lou Henson said. "He's beaten us every year. The last three years he's been a horse in there. He's devastating. He really killed us."

Missouri won its third straight game in this series, the last two by one point. The Tigers' struggle came in the second half this time.

Things looked under control when Finner gave Missouri a 61-48 lead with 12 minutes to play.

> "We've got the sick and wounded playing for us," Missouri coach Norm Stewart said. "I guess women and children were next."

Sophomore guard Richard Keene warmed up Illinois with consecutive three-pointers, then junior center Shelly Clark started connecting. Freshman point guard Kiwane Garris made two free throws with 4:49 left for a 66-65 Illinois lead. Missouri would be left to scramble for its existence until the unlikely crew of survivors took control in the third overtime.

"The second half, a couple of the overtimes, we had our drought," Stewart said. "We were into our 'prevent' offense."

After getting down 74-65, the Tigers concentrated on three-pointers.

Frazier and Atkins each made two around a 15-footer by Booker in the last 73 seconds of regulation.

"We really botched it toward the end there really badly," Henson said.

Crudup fouled out with 1:02 left. Frazier said he told Booker, "Now it's

up to us, the perimeter guys, to step up even more."

Frazier's three with four seconds left tied it at 79.

After Atkins and Finner fouled out in the first overtime, Thames scored Missouri's last two baskets of overtime.

Norm Stewart speaks to reporters at a postgame press conference in Columbia. (Columbia Daily Tribune)

Booker drove the middle, then dumped the ball off to Thames for one of his MU-record 13 assists.

Thames, who led Missouri with eight rebounds, dunked to tie the game at 88. Winfield committed his fifth foul as Garris drove the lane. With no time on the clock and the lane vacated, he had two free throws and needed only to make one to give Illinois the victory. He missed both.

"Basically, I just went up there and tried to get it over with," Garris said. "I just shot them poorly."

By that time, the tone of the game had changed in another way. Midway through the second half, Crudup was dominating Missouri's scoring while Illinois was well-balanced.

With some personnel moves dictated by the fouls, all five Tiger starters wound up in double figures as did the Illini starting five. Garris led all scorers with 31 points.

Illinois got 13 points from its reserves. Led by Sutherland's six, including the third overtime three-pointer that put MU ahead to stay, the Tigers got 17 points from the bench.

The Tigers won despite Illinois taking 23 more free throws and a 53-42 advantage on the boards.

Crudup virtually starred in one game, then stared at another from the bench.

"It was an important ballgame for us as far as our last game here, bragging rights," Crudup said.

"Especially for the seniors it was a game that we wanted to get out and play well."

Coach Stewart plots the team's next move during a break in the action. (Mike Stewart, Columbia Daily Tribune)

Booker said as much to the team on the floor when he fouled out with a 100-99 lead in the third overtime.

"I was telling them, 'This is my last time playing here. Don't lose it now,'" Booker said. "You can't feel tired in those type games. As bad as you really want to win, you have to just dig deeper and deeper."

After the first triple-overtime game for Missouri, the Tigers left satisfied. "That right there was one of the best games I've been in," Frazier said.

The series is scheduled to resume next year in the new Kiel Center.

"That's great to win the last one in the building," Stewart said.

The Tigers will leave with happy and extensive memories.

The year 1993 also saw Coach Stewart earn his 600th victory. His family congratulates him after the milestone win. (Karen Jackson, Columbia Daily Tribune)

Beyond the NORM

PERFECTO!

MARCH 6, 1994
David Holzman

For a team that has made an ironclad habit of winning, yesterday's game was out of the ordinary. Almost out of control.

In going 24-2 and undefeated in the Big Eight, the Tigers have become masters of the last few minutes. Yesterday, they couldn't seize command until the last very few seconds. Even then, if Eric Piatkowski's bomb at the buzzer had gone in, the Hearnes Center would have turned upside down. Missouri struggled to come from behind in an 80-78 victory over Nebraska and finish 14-0 in the Big Eight.

Trailing 78-77, Missouri came away from an intentional foul called on Eric Piatkowski without scoring. Piatkowski fouled Kelly Thames from behind as the Missouri freshman went up on a breakaway. Thames missed both free throws.

The Tigers retained possession because of the intentional foul. Melvin Booker drove, pulled up and banked in a jump shot, but it didn't count. Booker was called for charging by official Paul Janssen on the baseline. Erick Strickland, who was guarding Booker, was called for blocking by another official, Stanley Reynolds. The net effect: no basket,

> **Missouri struggled to come from behind in an 80-78 victory over Nebraska and finish 14-0 in the Big Eight.**

Missouri's ball with 16.6 seconds left under the alternating possession rule.

"I thought they were going to change it to a block," Booker said. "I was over there praying and begging, hoping they would change it to a block.

"They just gave us another chance. It kind of helped us out because so much time ran down. I made the basket with 12 seconds left, and Nebraska really didn't have time to set up the play they wanted to."

With 12.5 seconds left, Booker tried again. This time he made a layup plus a free throw after being fouled by Jamar Johnson. Three points the hard way gave Missouri its margin of victory.

"After they took my first one away, I wanted to get it and shoot it again, see if they're going to take that one away," Booker said.

Reynolds explained the seldom-seen double foul; Strickland's portion fouled him out.

"One official saw a player-control foul," Reynolds said. "One official saw a block. When that's the situation, we assess two fouls — a double foul. The possession goes to the possession arrow. Both of those fouls counted against the respective players."

Reynolds went to midcourt and emphatically made his point to Janssen. "It wasn't pleading a case," Reynolds said. "We were discussing what each official had."

Huffing and puffing their way to a comeback was standard fare in the first half of the season. Since they tried and failed at Notre Dame, the Tigers haven't lost. Most of the time, they've won going away.

"A lot of those games we went down to the buzzer," Lamont Frazier said.

"When we went down to the buzzer here, we were able to handle the situation like we did."

Stewart led his team to an 80-78 win over Nebraska to go 14-0 in the Big Eight in 1994. (Lisa D. Finger, Columbia Daily Tribune)

Coach Stewart turned the Missouri basketball program around from a 6-43 record in the two seasons before he took over as coach to a perennial postseason tournament team. His success brought increased media attention (above) and an undefeated Big Eight championship season with his 1994 squad, shown practicing on opposite page. (L.G. Patterson, Columbia Daily Tribune)

Beyond the NORM

EIGHT'S NOT ENOUGH

MARCH 25, 1994
Scott Cain

L OS ANGELES — Jevon Crudup huddled in a semicircle with family and friends, arms around each other, smiles putting off a thousand watts.

Flash.

The camera illuminated a small area behind the stands at the Los Angeles Sports Arena for a nanosecond, then the group disbanded only to reassemble moments later for another photo. Then another. And another.

If only Syracuse could have put as many bodies on Crudup and his low-post partner, Kelly Thames.

Though the guards commanded much of the attention last night, Missouri's inside combination tamed its counterpart and contributed significantly to MU's 98-88 NCAA West Region victory over Syracuse.

Crudup and Thames, a senior and freshman, respectively, combined for 34 points and 22 rebounds. Syracuse's John Wallace and Otis Hill, a sophomore and freshman, managed 16 points and 14 rebounds between them. Wallace's four turnovers were three more than Crudup and Thames had together.

> In the locker room, Missouri coach Norm Stewart told the players "to take it to the basket, just go up strong," Thames said.

Syracuse's two posts had been averaging a combined 31 points and 18 rebounds per game. They contributed less last night despite having an extra five-minute period.

"I just missed some easy shots," was all Wallace would say.

In three tournament games, Missouri has offered an inside force. Crudup had 19 points and 12 rebounds in the opener against Navy, and the Tigers shut down Wisconsin 7-footer Rashard Griffith in the second-round game.

So they expected the Orangemen to play a zone defense, if not to choke off the inside then at least to preserve their strength and a shallow bench. But Syracuse switched from zone to man-to-man and back again several times.

"Basically I just had to get inside and bang," Crudup said. "I knew they were going to play a lot of zone, but when they played man we just basically took advantage. We just had a lot of movement in our offense and were getting some good shots."

By halftime, the score was tied and so was the inside play. MU's duo had 13 points and nine rebounds, SU's duo 12 and eight.

In the locker room, Missouri coach Norm Stewart told the players "to take it to the basket, just go up strong," Thames said. "The first half we were struggling a bit."

Thames and Crudup dominated the rest of the way.

The only force that slowed either was a finger that intruded on Crudup's left eye late in overtime.

"A big finger," Crudup said.

The poke sent Crudup sprawling on the baseline, where he laid face down rubbing his eye for several moments. Finally, teammate Melvin Booker approached Crudup, saying, "Jevon, you've got to get up and go shoot the free throws."

By the time Crudup made one of the two free shots, Missouri led 90-83 with 1:53 left in OT and was on its way to the regional final.

Norm Stewart (right) reacts to the Tigers' overtime victory over Syracuse in the NCAA Round of 16. (Lisa D. Finger, Columbia Daily Tribune)

Beyond the NORM

HEAD TO HEAD

BOISE, Idaho — Norm Stewart and Bobby Knight do not look at tonight's game as a battle of wits between the over-50 crowd.

But when eighth-seeded Missouri and ninth-seeded Indiana tangle tonight in the opening round of the NCAA Tournament, the spotlight will be planted on two coaching legends facing each other for the first time. In a combined 64 years of coaching, they both have 659 victories. Only one will walk out of the Boise State Pavilion with 660.

"I told our squad, 'You know it's not between the coaches. It's between the players,'" Stewart said. "So that should be a lesser, in fact insignificant, part of it."

The players will determine who wins tonight, but their play is a reflection of the style and backgrounds of the coaches whose nicknames say it all —Stormin' Norman and The General.

Stewart is small-town crafty. The best athlete to come out of tiny Shelbyville, Missouri, he became a basketball and baseball star at MU. As a coach, he built a mediocre basketball program into a national

> "I told our squad, 'You know it's not between the coaches. It's between the players,'" Stewart said.

power, and in the process became the most recognizable person in the state.

He gets his share of blue chip recruits at Missouri, but his teams are often heavily populated with projects and role players who find a way to beat you.

After spending enough time with their coach, his players inherit Stewart's tenacious and sometimes ornery ways. As he said to an Oklahoma State fan who dared interfere with his postgame news conference earlier this year, "I can get combative." The fan, it should be noted, didn't care to take the 60-year-old Stewart up on the offer.

Knight might be even more combative. His transgressions against Puerto Rican police officers, reporters and folding chairs are legendary, but so are his graduation rates. In his 24-year career at Indiana, only two players who completed their eligibility have failed to graduate. And he wins. Knight has coached three national champions, 11 Big Ten champions, a

Pan-American gold-medal team and an Olympic champion.

Knight was not the athlete Stewart was. He sat on the bench for the Ohio State team that won the national championship in '60, but his teams reflect the discipline befitting a guy who got his coaching start at West Point at age 24.

Both coaches demand excellence from everyone around them — players, referees and media. When they don't get it, take cover.

"Two very animated characters," Missouri forward Julian Winfield said.

"They have a lot of wisdom between them.

"I think a couple times the players might be glancing over looking at the coaches trying to hear what they're talking about. I know the people right behind press row and right behind the benches will have a lot of fun watching those two. Those are two great coaches that have gotten a lot of national attention. It's great for college basketball."

It won't necessarily be great for the poor souls called upon to officiate tonight's game. Former Big Ten and Big Eight official Jim Bain has called his share of games involving both coaches. Bain said this game will probably provide a few war stories for the officials.

"It's probably those types of matchups that I miss most," Bain said. "That will be as exciting for the officials working that game as it would be to work a Final Four."

Can he recall a more volatile coaching matchup?

"I can recall a few of the games with Joe Cipriano and Norm being a little loud," he said.

Cipriano, the former Nebraska coach who once got Bain's attention during a game by firing a starter's pistol at Bain's rear end, was a mutual friend of Stewart and Knight. Stewart said he met the Indiana coach through Cipriano.

In the highly publicized matchup, all eyes were on Stormin' Norman and The General, but Stewart's focus was on winning the game. (Sean Meyers, Columbia Daily Tribune)

Although Knight wrote the foreword to Stewart's book on coaching, their paths have not crossed on the court. Missouri played Indiana 12 times from '54-'69 but the series ended then, two years before Knight took over the Hoosiers.

Stewart said the schools considered restarting the series in the late '80s but did not follow through on it.

Stewart has had one notable run-in with Knight, however.

In 1979, Stewart invited Knight to a coaching clinic at MU. A Missouri graduate assistant was supposed to take Knight to Columbia Regional Airport the following morning. The assistant overslept, so Stewart had to hurry Knight to Columbia Regional Airport himself.

"Stewart comes and picks me up in his pajamas," Knight said. "He has a jacket on, pajamas and bedroom slippers."

Knight caught the flight, connected in St. Louis and made it back to his destination of Warren, Ohio, in good shape. But he wanted to have a little fun with Stewart.

"I call my office and had my secretary call Stewart and tell him that I had missed the plane in St. Louis, I was able to get a flight for Pittsburgh, the Pittsburgh airport was fogged in, we had to overfly Pittsburgh to Philadelphia, and when I got to Philadelphia, the only way I could get to Warren was a Lear Jet," Knight said.

Sean Myers, Columbia Daily Tribune

He sent Stewart a bill for $1,200. To his surprise, he received a check from the Missouri athletic department.

"I got a little bit scared when I got that check," Knight said. "I thought, how long can they put me in jail for fraud?"

Knight then called MU athletic director Dave Hart. "I said, 'I just want you to know I tore up the check but don't say anything about it.' I sent Dave a membership in the Hoosier Booster Club, an Indiana license plate, stickers for the car, all kinds of crap and thanked Stewart and the basketball program for joining the Indiana Booster Club."

Afterwards, Knight waited patiently for retribution from Stewart. Stewart had his lawyer call Knight and tell him that he and his wife, Virginia, were getting a divorce — caused because Norm couldn't manage his money. Knight didn't bite.

But a few days later, Dan Rather called and wanted to talk to Knight for a "60 Minutes" segment. Thinking, for some reason, that Rather was an old military buddy of Stewart pulling a prank, Knight blew off Rather for three weeks.

Knight isn't always so playful, though. At the same MU coaching clinic in 1979, Missouri assistant coach George Scholz tried to have some fun at Knight's expense. Earlier in the summer, Knight was arrested on charges of aggravated assault for shoving a police officer in Puerto Rico during the Pan-Am

Games. He was convicted after leaving the country and still faces penalties if he returns. He was never extradited, however.

"I don't know much about extradition, but it's my understanding that once you're out of Indiana, they can order you back to Puerto Rico," Scholz said.

Knight angrily shot back: "I know a guy in Bayonne, N.J., who'll put bodies at the bottom of any river for 50 bucks. I told that policeman in Puerto Rico the same thing."

With that, Knight stalked out of the room.

Reporters who have covered the coaches can sympathize with Scholz. Stewart and Knight have tremendous senses of humor, but they dole out the jokes selectively to the media.

After surviving colon cancer and returning to coaching in the fall of 1989, Stewart had a chance to move into the role of lovable old curmudgeon with the media. But it just isn't in his nature. Although he was often charming with reporters as Missouri opened this season with an 18-3 record, his attitude has taken a turn for the paranoid since.

While Stewart ranks the media just above a pack of flesh-eating rats, he must bow to the master media basher — Knight.

"One thing peculiar about this game is I'm going to be the nice guy," Stewart said.

Knight, after all, once pulled a Cipriano and

fired a starter's pistol at a reporter. When he got off the plane in Boise yesterday, he took offense to a cameraman and began gently pushing him backwards.

So it should be no surprise that neither coach played the media's game this week. Neither wanted to talk about their own importance in their first clash or overplay their friendship.

"Jesus, are Stewart and I going to guard each other? Are we going to play 21? Are we going to play H-O-R-S-E?" Knight said.

Not always a media favorite, Stewart noted that "one thing peculiar about this game (against Bobby Knight's Hoosiers) is I'm going to be the nice guy." (Columbia Daily Tribune)

"Bobby and I have had an association, but I'm not sure how long it's been since we've talked," Stewart said.

Apparently the talking will not begin until tonight. Stewart was asked if he would call Knight and wish him good luck.

"No," Stewart replied crustily. "I hope he doesn't have good luck."

STEWART BESTS KNIGHT

Better erase those West Regional brackets.

Indiana won't be meeting UCLA in the second round. Missouri defeated the Hoosiers 65-60 last night in the opening round of the NCAA Tournament at the Boise State Pavilion.

With a makeshift lineup feeding off the energy of an inspired Norm Stewart, eighth-seeded Missouri advanced to the tournament's second round and will meet top-seeded UCLA.

—Joe Walljasper
March 18, 1995

Beyond the NORM

MISSOURI'S LUCK STOPS HERE

MARCH 20, 1995
Joe Walljasper

BOISE, Idaho — In 4.8 seconds, Tyus Edney served a reminder of how great and cruel basketball can be.

Playing their best game of the season, the eighth-seeded Missouri Tigers stood on the brink of the biggest upset of this NCAA Tournament and one of the biggest victories of Norm Stewart's career. And then Edney ripped it all away.

The UCLA senior went the length of the floor and laid in a shot over the outstretched hands of Derek Grimm. The buzzer sounded. The Bruins had escaped Missouri's scare and emerged with a 75-74 victory yesterday in the West Regional second round at the Boise State Pavilion.

Edney rode his teammates' shoulders off the court. On the other side, the Haley twins were face down on the floor. Julian Winfield wandered around the court with his hands clasped behind his head, a look of disbelief on his face.

"One point," UCLA coach Jim Harrick said. "It's crazy. It's a crazy business."

It is called March Madness, but it was simply

> Their best effort fell one point short. But it will surely be remembered as one of the greatest games in Missouri's history.

maddening for the Tigers, who seemed destined to win when freshman Kendrick Moore found Julian Winfield under the basket for a score in the waning seconds. UCLA called a timeout with 4.8 seconds left, leaving the Bruins just enough time for the game-winning shot.

The loss ended Missouri's season at 20-9. UCLA improved to 27-2 and will play Mississippi State in the regional semifinals.

Missouri's Paul O'Liney ended his college career with one of his best games.

He made five of six three-pointers and finished with 23 points. Grimm, who was so dehydrated from a bout with the flu that he had to take fluids intravenously before the game, made three of five three-point goals and scored 13. Jason Sutherland shook off a shooting slump and scored 15 points on four-of-eight shooting from behind the arc.

The Tigers did nearly everything they needed to win. They made a season-high 12 three-pointers on

19 attempts, made six of seven free throws and controlled UCLA's fast break.

Their best effort fell one point short. But it will surely be remembered as one of the greatest games in Missouri's history.

"I was watching a film on ESPN on the best games ever played," said UCLA senior Ed O'Bannon, who led all scorers with 24. "Maybe the next time they make a film like that, hopefully, this game will be on it."

Missouri might not be able to watch.

It will be tough to forget the day a young Missouri team almost eliminated the No. 1 team in the nation. Afterward, Stewart had very little to say to the media, but Moore said Stewart got his point across in a somber locker room.

"He told us we played our hearts out," Moore said.

Conventional wisdom had Missouri losing in the first round to ninth-seeded Indiana on Friday. Even after the Tigers beat the Hoosiers 65-60, few could have expected what they did yesterday against UCLA.

MU entered the game as a 12 1/2 point underdog. But Missouri quickly proved it wasn't intimidated, jumping to a 13-6 lead after four minutes of play.

The pressures of coaching in a down-to-the-wire game were nothing new for Stewart after three decades of coaching. (Columbia Daily Tribune)

Sutherland hit his first two three-pointers, and Winfield hit two twisting layups and a pair of free throws. The early lead came with an asterisk, however. Winfield picked up his third foul with 15:42 remaining and sat the rest of the half.

Without Winfield, Missouri didn't fold. The Tigers rode the precision of O'Liney's three-point shooting to a 42-34 halftime lead. O'Liney made all four of his three-point attempts and had 16 points before the break.

Missouri contained the Bruins' fast break in the first half, primarily because it made 54 percent of its shots.

Missouri continued its surge in the second half. When Sutherland and O'Liney hit consecutive three-pointers, the Tigers led 52-43 with 16:01 remaining in the game.

At that point, UCLA called a timeout and regrouped. The Bruins forced four quick turnovers, scored in transition and capped a 15-0 run with a three-pointer by Edney. That gave UCLA a 58-52 lead with 10:42 left.

"We thought after we went up by six that it was time to take control and play the way we're supposed to play," UCLA forward Charles O'Bannon said. "They fought back. They hit some threes. They made some free throws. They just wouldn't give up."

The Bruins held O'Liney in check in the final 10 minutes, but they couldn't contain Grimm. He scored 10 of his points in that span. His three-pointer with 3:50 left gave the Tigers a 72-69 lead.

Missouri went into a delay offense and failed to score on its next three possessions. Ed O'Bannon scored over Winfield and then added two free throws to give his team a 73-72 lead with 58.9 seconds remaining.

Missouri's possession was prolonged when UCLA's Cameron Dollar fouled Sutherland on a pick. The Tigers inbounded the ball again with 38.9 seconds left. Moore, who finished with 10 points, dribbled the ball in the backcourt until six seconds remained on the shot clock. He penetrated to the free throw line and jumped. He hung in the air for a moment and then found Winfield under the basket.

Winfield banked the ball in, sending the Missouri fans into a frenzy. UCLA quickly called timeout with 4.8 seconds left.

"In the huddle I heard Ed," Edney said. "He said, 'We're going to win.'"

Edney had just enough time to take the inbounds pass, negotiate his way upcourt against Sutherland, reverse his field with a behind-the-back dribble at midcourt, drive the right side of the lane and loop the ball high off the glass.

"It seemed like everything was going slow," Charles O'Bannon said. "It was like, are we going to win? Are we not? Are we going to win? Once he released the shot, it seemed like it rolled around the rim about eight times."

It didn't. It grazed the

front of the rim and fell in. Missouri's season was over before the ball hit the ground.

"We played a heck of a ballgame," Winfield said. "We did the things we were supposed to do. It came down to the last shot, and UCLA hit that shot. Of course nobody's too happy about that, but we had a heck of a season."

Despite the tournament loss to UCLA, the Tigers' 1994 undefeated Big Eight season will always be remembered as one of Coach Stewart's greatest accomplishments. (Lisa D. Finger, Columbia Daily Tribune)

Beyond the NORM

STEWART NEARS MILESTONE

FEBRUARY 3, 1996
Joe Walljasper

It is being treated like any other, but Norm Stewart will be coaching a historic game today.

When Missouri (13-7, 3-3 Big Eight) and Oklahoma (11-8, 2-4) play at Lloyd Noble Arena, Stewart will coach his 1,000th game.

To say Stewart isn't putting any added emphasis on the game would be an understatement. MU assistant coach Kim Anderson wasn't sure what the exact milestone was until he was told.

"He likes to win every game, whether it's No. 1 or 500 or 1,000," Anderson said.

As far as Stewart is concerned, the less said about this 1,000th-game business the better. For the third straight week, Stewart canceled his "weekly" press conference. He did not return *Tribune* phone calls.

In lieu of actual conversation, a news release was issued. On coaching his 1,000th game, Stewart is quoted as saying: "It just makes people realize how

Stewart has coached through eight presidencies —John F. Kennedy to Bill Clinton—and was even honored by the latter for his work with the Coaches vs. Cancer charity.

old you are. It's funny because you really don't keep track of things like that until someone points it out to you. If I did, I would be teaching history and not coaching basketball."

Whether the 61-year-old Stewart wants to acknowledge it or not, the 1,000-game plateau is a major honor. You don't stick around for that long without winning.

Among active coaches, only North Carolina's Dean Smith and Mount St. Mary's Jim Phelan have coached as many games. Stewart will be the 10th Division I coach to break 1,000.

"In today's college environment, there are very few people who are able to accomplish that feat," Anderson said. "It says a lot for him as a person and a teacher that he has been able to adjust to a lot of situations and been able to adjust to the game. I mean, he's put together successful teams for what, 35 years."

In 1961, when Stewart began as the 26-year-old coach at Northern Iowa, a burger, fries and shake at McDonald's cost 45 cents.

Stewart has coached through eight presidencies — John F. Kennedy to Bill Clinton — and was even honored by the latter for his work with the Coaches vs. Cancer charity. Stewart, himself, has presided over 673 victories and 326 defeats.

After time runs out on the Tigers and Sooners today, he will have one more in the W or L column.

It is one game amongst 999 others, but for two hours today it will be the most important one of his career. The setting is ironic, considering that seven years ago Stewart's life, not to mention his coaching career, was in a precarious position after he collapsed on the team flight to Norman, Oklahoma.

He overcame the cancer that was diagnosed at that time. He has overcome about every other imaginable obstacle, too.

Missouri was 6-43 in the two seasons before his arrival in 1967. He built a winning team in just two years. His teams won four straight Big Eight titles from 1980-83. After running afoul of the NCAA, he has rebuilt a winner in the '90s, taking his last four teams to the NCAA Tournament.

In a profession full of nomads, Stewart has endured at Missouri for 29 seasons. The average stint of Big Eight coaches who have joined the league since Stewart is 5.2 years. He broke in at MU as a contemporary of Henry Iba and Tex Winter. Now Stewart is competing against Tim Floyd and Ricardo Patton.

After 1,000 games, Coach Stewart still puts on his "game face" for every contest. (Brian W. Kratzer, Columbia Daily Tribune)

Times have changed, and Stewart has changed with them — to a degree. He still runs the same offense and man-to-man defense that he's used since the '60s, but he has made allowances for the '80s innovations of the shot clock and three-point line.

Some would argue that Stewart has mellowed a little since his bout with cancer. Some would argue that he hasn't.

"That subject's been brought up, but I just don't see a significant change," said Jim Kennedy, who played for Stewart in the mid-70s and now serves as color commentator on Tiger radio broadcasts.

"Of course when you age from late 30s to 61 you might soften your perspectives on some things. But as far as competitiveness, which is the root of everything, I don't see a change at all."

Among the many highlights in Coach Stewart's 1,000 games was the Tigers' championship victory over Kansas State in 1971. Sharing the Big 8 trophy with Stewart are co-captains Mike Griffin (left) and Greg Flaker. (Columbia Daily Tribune)

During his career, Coach Stewart had many a sideline chat with the men in pinstripes. (Sean Meyers, Columbia Daily Tribune)

Beyond the NORM

FLIPPIN' THE BIRDS

FEBRUARY 5, 1997
Matt Schuckman

There was an impassioned coach, barking up and down the sideline, never allowing his team to lose belief in itself or the belief it could upset the nation's No. 1-ranked team.

There was the consummate role player, finding himself with the game in his hands and knocking down a 16-foot jumper, a shot he threw up to beat an expiring shot clock.

And there were those mysterious Missouri Tigers, the same ones who seemed aloof just one week ago, celebrating one of the most remarkable upsets in their storied rivalry with the Kansas Jayhawks.

In front of a raucous crowd of nearly 14,000 at the Hearnes Center, the Tigers did the unthinkable, they found a vulnerability in the top-ranked and undefeated Jayhawks, defeating them 96-94 in double overtime last night.

"No one expected this, except maybe the players and the coaches," said MU senior guard Corey Tate. "No one except us, but we believed."

And it was Tate, who finished with 14 points, making the shot of his career with the game on the

> "No one expected this, except maybe the players and the coaches," said MU senior guard Corey Tate. "No one except us, but we believed."

line.

Tied at 94 with less than 30 seconds to play in the second overtime, the Tigers (12-10, 4-6 Big 12) reversed the ball to Tyron Lee on the left wing.

Missouri cleared out, giving Lee the option to go one-on-one with KU's Jerod Haase.

However, Kansas guard Jacque Vaughn stepped in and stripped the ball. As Lee and Vaughn fought for possession, the ball squirted free and right to Tate, standing two steps behind the free throw line. He quickly set himself, shooting as the shot clock ticked down to three.

The shot caught nothing but net, leaving the Jayhawks (22-1, 8-1) just 5.6 seconds for a final scoring chance.

"We run the scramble," MU coach Norm Stewart said. "We knew where we wanted to go with the ball on the scramble. We got it there. You don't know who's going to shoot it because you can't pick that, but we knew where we wanted it.

"We got it there, and he got the shot and he knocked it in."

On KU's final series, MU's defense forced Haase to bring the ball up the right side of the court and dish to Raef LaFrentz at the top of the key. LaFrentz's desperation three-pointer clanked off the right side of the backboard, but it's uncertain whether it would have counted had it been good.

The loss ended Kansas' unbeaten streak at 22 games and marked the third time in the 1990s that MU has beaten a No. 1-ranked KU team. The Tigers upset the Jayhawks 77-71 in Lawrence and 95-87 in Columbia in 1990. Both times Missouri was ranked in the top five.

It is the second straight season Missouri has handed Kansas its first conference loss and the third straight season the Jayhawks have lost in Columbia.

"I've said a million times it was unrealistic," KU coach Roy Williams said of his team's bid to finish the schedule undefeated. "I never talked in those terms, never wanted to think about that, because I knew it wouldn't happen."

It could have lasted one more night if Missouri had folded after giving up a three-point lead late in regulation.

The Tigers went up 71-68 when Derek Grimm, who missed two of four free throws in the final 26 seconds, made the second of two free throws with 13.5 seconds to play. The Tigers immediately fouled Vaughn in the frontcourt, taking away a chance for a three-pointer.

Vaughn made the first free throw but missed the second. It caromed off the right side of the rim. LaFrentz, who led all scorers with 26 points, slipped inside Grimm with a hook move, grabbed the rebound and laid in the game-tying basket.

Dibi Ray had a chance to win the game at the buzzer, but his 16-foot runner bounced long.

"I thought that was the toughest hill we had to climb because we had the ballgame won," Stewart said. "That could have been curtains."

Missouri didn't wilt, making all 12 free throw attempts in the first overtime, including two by Tate with 10 seconds to play that forced a second overtime.

In the second overtime, Billy Thomas gave KU a quick boost, knocking down a three-pointer from the left wing for

The KU crowd taunts Coach Stewart, but to no avail as Missouri defeated top-ranked KU 96-94 in double overtime. (Sean Meyers, Columbia Daily Tribune)

an 89-86 lead. But, with the shot clock winding down, MU's Jason Sutherland answered with a three-pointer ... from deep in the right corner ... from behind the backboard ... that he shot from his hip.

It was the play that finally broke KU's spirits.

"We defend and really do a good job on Jason's three-pointer," Williams said. "That was a huge basket for them."

The teams traded baskets and free throws before L. Dee Murdock came off the bench to knock down a hook shot over the foul-prone LaFrentz with 47.2 seconds left. Vaughn answered, driving down the lane with a running hook shot that tied the game at 94 and set up Tate's heroics.

Junior forward Kelly Thames led Missouri with 24 points, while Grimm added 20 and Sutherland 18. But it was Missouri's presence on the boards that made the difference.

The Tigers outrebounded the Jayhawks 43-37, getting 11 from Thames, six from Grimm and five each from Tate and Ray. It was that physical presence that kept Kansas from making its patented scoring run.

"For our guys," Stewart said, "it was their night."

Stewart talks with Kansas head coach Roy Williams (right) and KU assistant coach Matt Doherty (left), who was named the head coach at Notre Dame after the 1998-99 season. (Sean Meyers, Columbia Daily Tribune)

The MU-KU rivalry has generated many great memories. Above, Stewart congratulates player Lee Coward in 1987 after beating Kansas for the second time that year. (Columbia Daily Tribune)

CHAPTER 4

Beyond the NORM

THREE-POINT ATTACK

OCTOBER 27, 1994
Scott Cain

BEYOND THE BENCH

W hen the Missouri basketball team deposited 164 three-point goals last season, it did more than set a school record. The buckets also helped deposit a princely sum toward cancer research.

Coach Norm Stewart's Three-Point Attack, a fundraising program administered by the American Cancer Society, generated $148,000 in new donations for research, education and patient services.

The program started last year after the National Association of Basketball Coaches formed a partnership with the American Cancer Society and called it Coaches vs. Cancer.

In the Three-Point Attack, businesses and individuals pledge an amount of money for every three-pointer the Tigers make.

The program began at seven schools in Missouri. But there is a reasonable limit on how many three-point goals a few players can collect, so they've applied the full-court press this

season—they've taken the program nationwide.

Organizers set a goal of involving 100 schools this year. Already, more than 90 have agreed to participate, and Stewart said they expect to have 100 when the season opens next month.

"This program has great potential," Stewart said.

Yes, even more potential than the exponential growth that occurred this year.

Consider that even though almost 100 schools are participating, NCAA Division I basketball comprises 209 programs. The American Cancer Society just doesn't have enough staff to contact and work with every school right now.

But they plan to expand as time and resources allow.

The rush to aid the fight says

something about how devastating and firm a grip cancer has on so many people.

Cancer will kill an estimated half million Americans this year, and more than 27,000 new cases will be diagnosed in Missouri alone, according to the ACS.

The faces on those deaths and new cases will belong to the elderly and to the young. The disease does not discriminate by race or physical condition. Cancer strikes cab drivers, computer programmers, the doctors who treat it, housewives, entertainers, mechanics and basketball coaches.

Stewart was diagnosed with colon cancer in February, 1989 a few days after collapsing on a flight to a game in Norman, Oklahoma. He beat the illness through treatment and courage, and he returned to coach the next season.

Some coaches affected by cancer have been as fortunate. Some have not. Joe B. Hall, the legendary former coach at Kentucky, was diagnosed with colon cancer six months before Stewart and overcame it. Arkansas coach Nolan Richardson lost a daughter to leukemia seven years ago. And Jim Valvano, whose North Carolina State team stunned Houston in the 1983 championship game, succumbed to cancer 18 months ago.

Norm Stewart holds his first press conference after recovering from cancer surgery on October 24, 1989. (Columbia Daily Tribune)

Stewart talked with Valvano after Valvano had been diagnosed, one ex-cancer patient to a hopeful one.

"I don't think I could have done it if I had not had cancer," Stewart said.

Stewart lends an ear or morsels of advice to cancer patients still, remembering often something that Hall told him in '89: "Do not answer the phone. Don't talk to anybody you don't want to talk to."

"I try to pass that along to other people," Stewart said.

And now almost 100 other coaches are passing along their help, too. Among the participants are Richardson, Mike Krzyzewski of Duke, Eddie Sutton of Oklahoma State, Roy Williams of Kansas, Gene Keady of Purdue, Lon Kruger of Florida and Lute Olson of Arizona.

ROAST AND TOAST

SEPTEMBER 7, 1995
Joe Walljasper

KANSAS CITY — It's a rare day that folksy Kansas basketball coach Roy Williams and cantankerous Missouri coach Norm Stewart can find a common bond.

On January nights, it might as well be the Hatfields vs. McCoys when Stewart and Williams meet at the Hearnes Center or Allen Fieldhouse. Last night, they sat together in front of a bi-partisan audience and had one thing in common—they were taking a verbal beating from their colleagues.

"They asked me to roast Norm Stewart and Roy Williams . . . . That's like roasting the Pope and Al Capone," former Iowa State coach Johnny Orr cackled. "And I know damn well you know who's who."

As a benefit for the Coaches vs. Cancer charity, Williams and Stewart offered themselves up for abuse at a "Roast and Toast" at the Westin Crown Center.

The abuse flowed from a panel that included current and former coaches George Raveling, Bill Raftery, P.J. Carlisimo, Abe Lemons, Orr and Charlie Spoonhour. Duke's Mike Krzyzewski was scheduled to attend but, because of his ailing back, was forced to send his insults by videotape.

> "They asked me to roast Norm Stewart and Roy Williams . . . . That's like roasting the Pope and Al Capone," former Iowa State coach Johnny Orr cackled.

And in the name of charity and coaching brotherhood, Stewart and Williams laughed together like old buddies.

"It's unparalleled to have these two gentlemen sitting next to each other, chatting as if they were friends and like each other," Carlisimo deadpanned. "There's a joint meeting of the Norm Stewart Fan Club, Lawrence, Kansas, Chapter and the Roy Williams Fan Club, Columbia, Missouri, Chapter being held later in a phone booth downstairs."

The roasters touched on Stewart's finer points.

His looks.

"He's a sex symbol for women who no longer care," Lemons said.

His personality.

"Norm lights up a room by leaving it," Raftery said.

His education.

"Norm attended Shelbyville Grammar School, Shelbyville High School and the University of

Norm Stewart and Kansas Coach Roy Williams (right) formed a temporary alliance as they were both "roasted" to benefit Coaches vs. Cancer. (Sean Meyers, Columbia Daily Tribune)

Missouri, which was a very convenient arrangement since they used the same textbooks at all three," Carlisimo said.

His former girlfriends.

"They showed me a picture of Helga, that was Norm's steady. She had so much hair under her arms it looked like she had Buckwheat in a headlock," Spoonhour said.

His student-athletes.

"People say Norm is tough on his players. I take exception to that. I can substantiate his numerous visits to halfway houses to check on his players," Raftery said.

As expected, the irreverent and often incoherent

Norm Stewart proved he was a good sport when he was roasted by fellow coaches who hit on everything from Stewart's former girlfriends to his looks. (Columbia Daily Tribune)

Tennis great Arthur Ashe and Norm Stewart are honored on the football field in Columbia in 1975. Ashe, who won Wimbleton that year and is orginally from St. Louis, was to be inducted into the Missouri Sports Hall of Fame in 1975.

University of Missouri Sports Information

rr was a hoot. He began by grousing that because there ere women in the crowd, "I had to change my whole damn eech."

He recalled his first meeting with Williams.

"When they hired Roy Williams, I said, 'Look at that ce-looking young man. Isn't that a nice-looking young an?'" Orr said. "'He looks like a little nice kid to me.'

"I go down there, and we're behind 90-50. There's three inutes to go, and I finally decide we're going to lose this me, so I subbed. As I subbed, he subbed. But he put his st team back in there.

"When we came to shake hands I said, 'Damn, Roy, you t a one-year contract?'

"He said, 'Don't take it personally, that's just the way the bstitution order came.' I said, '... Make an exception.' "

Stewart and Williams were allowed rebuttals at the end the roast and fired a few shots back at the roasters.

Stewart, vowing to be the only speaker to finish in less than the assigned seven minutes because his bladder was calling, thanked the American Cancer Society's Jerry Quick, who helped him begin the Coaches vs. Cancer Three-Point Challenge.

Williams relied on his trademark banter—you guessed it—tedious golf stories.

Williams and Stewart showed that they have more in common than might be expected. Both of their lives have been touched by cancer. Williams lost his mother to the disease, and Stewart battled back from colon cancer in 1989. And they expressed that if not best friends, they share a professional admiration for each other.

"I'm not going to say that during the 40 minutes we play that I like him," Williams said, "but I do respect him and the job he's done."

Beyond the NORM

SIGNS STOLEN

FEBRUARY 10, 1994
Scott Cain

Nobody is quite sure when they disappeared. All that the residents of Shelbyville know is the two signs are gone—the ones proclaiming their northeast Missouri community as the hometown of MU basketball coach Norm Stewart.

Presumably, the signs were stolen as a prank, several residents said. Nobody's sure who the culprits were, though everybody has a theory.

"Our first thought was Billy Tubbs," longtime resident Connie Ray said, laughing. The Oklahoma coach and Stewart are noted Big Eight rivals.

A more likely scenario is that college students pilfered the pseudo-landmarks.

The two signs used to greet folks entering town from the north and south on Highway 15. They were erected to honor Stewart about 10 years ago, said Ray, on whose land one of the signs stood.

Stewart was born and reared in Shelbyville, population 645, about 75 miles northeast of Columbia.

Stewart and Oklahoma coach Billy Tubbs after Missouri's 93-90 victory over OU in 1988. (Columbia Daily Tribune)

"... Probably some of the guys that belong to the SWDAC probably took it down for posterity," Stewart said, "and they're getting ready to put it in the hall of fame of the SWDAC."

The SWDAC was a group of high school buddies in Stewart's day, an "athletic club," he called them.

Now, without the signs as proof, there is at least one doubter to Stewart's Shelbyville connection.

"My granddaughter was telling a little boy at school that Norm Stewart was from Shelbyville," mayor Jerome Vangels said. "The boy wouldn't believe it. So she said she would take a picture of it to prove it to him. My wife and granddaughter went to take a picture of the signs, and there weren't any signs. Apparently, they'd been gone for some time."

Residents estimate the north sign vanished in December. The south sign disappeared a few months earlier. Everybody assumed at first that they had been taken down for repainting by the Shelbyville Civic Club, which paid to have them put up originally.

But Ray and her husband, Donnie, knew the north sign had been stolen when they inspected the site around Christmas. Both posts were broken, and a crescent wrench, possibly used to unbolt the signs, was left.

The signs measure four feet by eight feet, Donnie Ray said.

Though no formal complaint has been filed, Shelby County sheriff Gerald Gander said he prob-ably will fill out a report after contacting the Civic Club.

The Rays own a business on the north end of town that sells petroleum and propane to farmers. Connie Ray said they purchased the business from Stewart's father, Ken, in 1967. They remain loyal Tiger fans, like many of Shelbyville's residents.

"We have some people here in Shelbyville who follow them wherever they go," the mayor said.

No plans have been made to replace the signs, but Connie Ray said, "I'm sure somebody will put some back up."

In the meantime, Gander said he will keep his ears open.

"Eventually we'll know" who stole the signs, Gander said. "Somebody will talk too much. Young people like to brag."

Stewart's basketball roots go back to his hometown of Shelbyville, Missouri, where he played for the Shelbyville High basketball team. Norm (33) is shown here in the first row with his teammates from the 1952 state runner-up team. (Photo courtesy of University of Missouri Sports Information)

Beyond the NORM

OUTSTANDING CITIZEN OF THE YEAR

JUNE 15, 1994
Dan Fitzpatrick

L ast night, Missouri basketball coach Norm Stewart had a mouthful of carrot cake when he heard the news.

In fact, when Stewart took the podium at the Columbia Chamber of Commerce's annual awards banquet to accept his Outstanding Citizen of the Year Award, he was one of the few in the audience who was surprised.

"If I had known this was going to happen, I would have worn a suit," Stewart told 300 chamber members, his dark blazer framing a polka-dot tie.

It's been a heady past couple of months for Stewart. First came the Tigers' undefeated Big Eight season and the AP's Coach of the Year Award. Then, Stewart stood in the Oval Office and accepted the American Cancer Society's "Courage Award" from President Bill Clinton. Stewart had a bout with colon cancer in 1989, and since then, Stewart-sponsored programs have raised hundreds of thousands of dollars for cancer research. Stewart's wife, Virginia, who knew about the chamber award but

> " . . . Probably some of the guys that belong to the SWDAC probably took it down for posterity," Stewart said.

kept it a secret for three weeks, said last night, "I think it is so much more important that people in your own community recognize you."

Friends, family and former Missouri players say an award that honors Stormin' Norman's high level of service to the community is long overdue. True, while some of his players had high-profile legal troubles while in school, most quietly emerged from Stewart's program as integral parts of the community.

Many of these players were strong-willed to begin with, but some attribute their success away from the basketball court to Stewart's one-on-one, fatherly coaching style.

"His biggest contribution is what he teaches you about life," says Al Eberhard, who played for Stewart between 1970 and 1974 and went on to play professional basketball with the Detroit Pistons. Eberhard is now corporate and capital development adminis-trator for the University of Missouri-Columbia Athletic Department.

Eberhard still remembers "the talk" and what it did for his psyche. "I wasn't reaching my potential in the classroom, so Norm and I sat down and had a heart-to-heart talk," he said. "It made me reassess my priorities. We joke about it now, but it was a tremen-dous help to me at the time."

Former Missouri basketball player Jon Sundvold said Stewart is an honest man who demands a lot from his players. This, Sundvold said, translates to life after basket-ball.

"When you play basketball for Norm, you learn a lot about yourself," said Sundvold, who after nine years in the NBA decided to pursue a career as an investment consult-ant. He now works with BC Christopher, a securities broker in Columbia.

When Coach Stewart took the podium at the Columbia Chamber of Commerce's annual awards banquet to accept his Outstanding Citizen of the Year Award, he was one of the few in the audience who was surprised. Pictured with Stewart are his wife, Virginia (left), and his daughter, Laura. (L. G. Patterson, Columbia Daily Tribune)

Beyond the NORM

ONE FOR THE AGES

Stewart Continues Tradition of Building Winners

NOVEMBER 29, 1994
Melinda Via

RETIREMENT

N orm Stewart doesn't have an old, discolored calendar still turned to that day in 1967 when MU athletic director Dan Devine brought him back to Missouri to resurrect an aching basketball program.

He doesn't often realize the time that has elapsed, but every now and again there are reminders.

The butch haircut, now called a buzz, has been a fad three times since Stewart began pacing in front of the Tigers' bench.

Every year, for the past 28, Stewart invites coaches to Columbia for his coaching clinic. One of this year's guests was Gene Bartow, who Stewart remembers talking with 18 years ago when

And when will the dean of the Big Eight step down? Stewart doesn't have a date set, but he promises he will leave eventually.

Bartow took over the Alabama-Birmingham program.

"You don't really think about it, but we were just talking about how good we felt," Stewart said after the clinic late last month. "Today, people are living longer, but I got started so early in this business. I was coaching when I was 22.

"I do have to admit, sometimes some things creep in, but I just try to make sure it's today."

Stewart, 59, watched this year as three coaches left the Big Eight. That brought the number of coaching changes in the league to 35 during Stewart's tenure.

Norm Stewart plays golf during the annual Missouri Tiger Invitational Golf Tournament. (Columbia Daily Tribune)

And when will the dean of the Big Eight step down? Stewart doesn't have a date set, but he promises he will leave eventually.

"I don't see it happening for awhile," said assistant Kim Anderson, who also played for Stewart from 1974-77. "He feels good. He enjoys coaching. His energy level is great. He loves to compete, and there's no better place to compete than on the court.

"I think he likes challenges, and this team is a challenge. Last year's was, too."

Ah, last year. A 28-4 season. A 14-0 Big Eight record, only the third Big Eight school to accomplish a perfect season and the first since 1971. National Coach of the Year honors.

The only part of the past season that could have been any better would've been one more victory, which would have sent the Tigers into the Final Four of the NCAA Tournament for the first time ever.

Is that it? Is that what keeps a man at the same university for 28 seasons?

Stewart has led 14 teams to the NCAA Tournament, twice making the Elite Eight but never the Final Four. It is, perhaps, the only milestone he has not reached.

"We have a chance at Missouri to do that, we can do that" he said, without saying if that's what he would base his retirement on. "On the foundation that we're on now, it is not impossible. When I first came here, it was not impossible, but the probability was minimal. Now the foundation is good enough that we can do that. That's what we're striving to do."

Peers wonder, but aren't surprised, at Stewart's longevity.

"In this day and age, if you got started right now, I don't know that you could ever get it done," said Rich Daly, Stewart's assistant and recruiting guru.

"I've been here 12 years, and that feels like forever." Administrators and assistant coaches say what drives Stewart on and off the court is his competitiveness.

"Coaching at this level takes an inordinate amount of mental toughness," MU athletic director Joe Castiglione said. "That's why Norm has an edge, he has that mental toughness...

"He's a competitor supreme, and he's good. It's not easy to be good." It might be cards on a plane trip to a game, a round of golf, shooting pool or just a debate.

"You always know where Norm stands," Castiglione said. "You don't have to sit there and guess what he thinks about a certain subject. People may not like it, but he'll let his opinion be known."

To those outsiders who think Stewart is tough, he is, said Daly.

"We've had differences, but he's one of those fellas who, when you work for him, you know what he expects from you and if you do that and do it in the right way you won't have any problems," Daly said. "He'll listen, but we all know he's the boss. Whatever he says goes. He doesn't tell you one thing and do something else."

In 1967, Devine needed someone for the long term, someone to turn the sagging basketball program around and walk it to national prominence.

Stewart was coaching at State College of Iowa, now Northern Iowa, at the time, and in six seasons there he had compiled a 97-42 record.

Missouri had won six of 49 games in the previous two seasons.

"He epitomized what I thought a Missouri coach should be—young, dynamic and preferably a Mis-

> "Coaching at this level takes an inordinate amount of mental toughness," MU athletic director Joe Castiglione said. "That's why Norm has an edge, he has that mental toughness...

souri kid because we wanted to strengthen the program's image in the state," Devine said.

Stewart, a native of Shelbyville, had played for the Tigers only 11 years earlier. He led the Big Seven conference in scoring with a 24.1 average and was an All-American in 1956, and according to Anderson, "He can still shoot that baby."

When he returned to coach at 32, he felt he had an image problem.

"When I first started, when I came back, people still saw me as the player even though I'd been out of school 11 years," Stewart said. "I had that feeling, maybe I was incorrect. But I had that feeling, 'Well, they're still judging me on the basis of being a player.' Now, most people don't even realize I went to school here."

Stewart's Tigers went 10-16 his first year, but "we won the second year and we've been winning since," Stewart said. Actually, he's had four losing seasons.

"Sure, it would be easy for me to say I envisioned he would stay this long when I hired him," Devine said. "Well, I didn't expect him to win as many conference championships and set records like he has, but I knew that if we could get him a nice place to play that he would be happy at Missouri."

The Hearnes Center opened in 1972, replacing Brewer Fieldhouse as the Tigers' home.

It wasn't until Stewart's ninth season that the Tigers won a league title and advanced to the NCAA Tournament, although several teams had played in the NIT.

"Most coaches don't get a lot of -respect early in their careers," said Anderson, a member of that first championship team. "But once he won the first championship, and then once he won four in a row, I don't think respect has ever been a problem."

With 731 career victories to his name, Norm Stewart flashed many postgame smiles. (Sean Meyers, Columbia Daily Tribune)

Beyond the NORM

STEWART LEAVES LONG LEGACY BEHIND

APRIL 1, 1999
James D. Horne

H e's been a constant fixture at the University of Missouri, and after 32 years of service, Missouri coach Norm Stewart will give up his spot on the sidelines.

Stewart announced his retirement this morning at a press conference at the Hearnes Center.

Affectionately called "Stormin' Norman," Stewart has been one of the most successful college basketball coaches of all time. Stewart started his coaching career as an assistant with Missouri (1957-61) and moved on to become the head coach at State College of Iowa (Northern Iowa, 1961-67). The next year Stewart was hired to become Missouri's skipper and that's where he remained for the next 32 years.

During that time, Stewart won 731 games (634 at Missouri) and is the seventh most-winningest coach of all-time. The only coaches who have won more games are Dean Smith (879), Adolph Rupp (876), Henry Iba (767), Ed Diddle (759), Phog Allen (746) and Bobby Knight (742).

> "Coach Stewart has done an outstanding job while at Missouri," said former MU assistant Gary Filbert yesterday. "He sold basketball to the State of Missouri and has done a lot for it in his time here."

"Coach Stewart has done an outstanding job while at Missouri," said former MU assistant Gary Filbert yesterday. "He sold basketball to the state of Missouri and has done a lot for it in his time here."

Stewart's resume is impressive. Stewart won more Big 12/Eight games (257) and conference tournaments (six) than any other coach, and his eight regular season championships tie him with former Kansas State coach Tex Winter for second in Big Eight history behind Allen's 24.

The only coaches that have coached longer at a school than Stewart were Allen, who coached at Kansas for 39 years, and Iba, who led Oklahoma State for 36 years.

"Norm is a credit to his game and his profession," former Oklahoma State coach Henry Iba said in Stewart's book *Stormin' Back*. "It was a challenge to compete with him and it's been a pleasure to have him as a friend."

Before Stewart joined Missouri, the Tigers had never won more than 20 games in a season. Prior to his becoming coach, Missouri had only won 630 games in 60 years (1907-67). With Stewart at the helm, Missouri won 20 games 17 times and he has won four more games in 32 seasons than the 14 coaches before him did.

Stewart led Missouri to 16 NCAA Tournaments and five berths in the NIT, including this year's first-round loss to New Mexico. Missouri has advanced to the Elite Eight twice and the Sweet 16 once. Before Stewart, Missouri only had one postseason bid in the 1944 NCAA Tournament.

Stewart was also named national coach of the year by six different organizations.

"There's no question that his peers and other coaches have great respect for him," Filbert said. "It was so tough to get other schools to come into the Hearnes Center and play."

But for all of Stewart's peaks, there have been many valleys. Stewart has never won a national championship

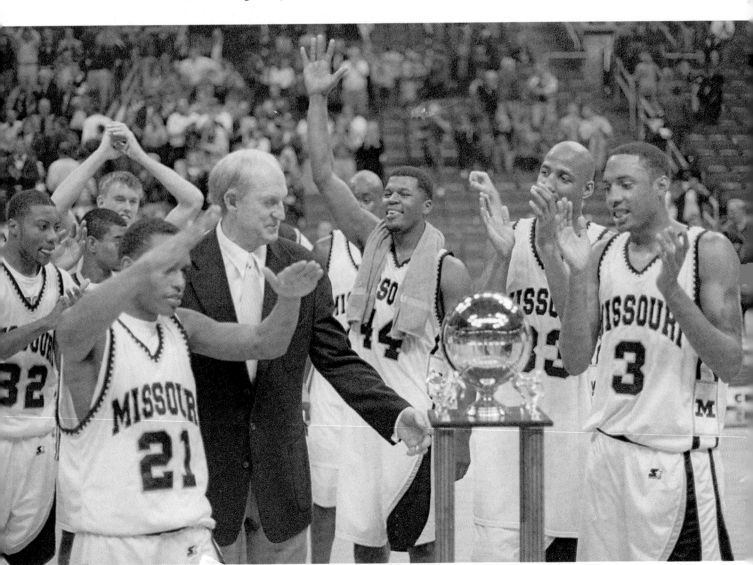

Norm Stewart is surrounded by Tigers celebrating Missouri's victory over Illinois in St. Louis in 1997. (R.C. Adams, Columbia Daily Tribune)

and developed a history of early exits in the NCAAs. Missouri was knocked out in the first round of the NCAA Tournament eight times and only advanced to the second round three times.

This season was especially hard. After finishing second in the Big 12 Tournament and receiving a first-round bye, Missouri was knocked off by Kansas State.

Then after getting back into the NCAAs for the first time in four years, Missouri was shocked by New Mexico's last-second game-winning shot in the first round of the West Regional.

"It's hard right now, and not for me, it's hard for the players," Stewart said after the Tigers' exit from this year's tournament.

Stewart played basketball and baseball for three years (1954-56) at Missouri. While on the basketball team, Stewart was captain his junior and senior seasons and led the Big Seven Conference in scoring during the 1955-56 season, averaging 24.1 points a game. He was named a Helms Foundation All-American after the season. Stewart scored 1,124 points in his career, which ranks him 22nd all-time.

Stewart was also the top pitcher of the Tiger baseball team that won the 1954 NCAA Championship.

Stewart signed contracts to play with the NBA's St. Louis Hawks and in the minor league system of baseball's Baltimore Orioles. He spent one year with both the Hawks and Orioles before returning to Missouri as an assistant.

But the biggest battle Stewart ever won was surviving cancer in 1989. After collapsing on a flight to Oklahoma to play the Sooners, Stewart was diagnosed with colon cancer and a diseased gall bladder. Stewart beat the disease and went on to start a cancer program, "Three-Point Attack: Norm's Special Challenge," for the American Cancer Society in 1990.

That program turned into the nationwide "Coaches vs. Cancer" program sponsored by the National Basketball Coaches Association in 1991. More than 100 schools have participated in the program and Stewart was honored by President Bill Clinton in 1994 for his efforts.

Stewart grew up in Shelbyville as the youngest of four children. Stewart graduated from a class of 16 and didn't have indoor plumbing until his senior year of high school.

"Coach Stewart is one of the finest competitors in all of collegiate basketball and has the ability to instill that drive to his ballclub after he's provided them with excellent individual and team fundamentals," said CBS analyst Billy Packer in Stewart's book *Stormin' Back.*

But everything that Stewart is and has become will now be left to the history books, because this "Storm" has finally passed by.

> "It's hard right now, and not for me, it's hard for the players," Stewart said after the Tigers' exit from this year's tournament.

Coach Stewart (center) talks with his current players prior to announcing his retirement. (Sean Meyers, Columbia Daily Tribune)

Beyond the NORM

RIVALS REMEMBER "THE DEAN"

APRIL 1, 1999
Russ Baer

T he Dean is stepping down from his post, leaving his students with a mixed bag of emotions.

Norm Stewart, dubbed the dean of coaches in the Big 12, announced his retirement this morning, and his former coaching colleagues were quick to pay homage to their long-time mentor.

Several of Stewart's "students" paid their respects to the teacher who introduced them to Big Eight—and more recently—Big 12 basketball over his 32-year coaching career at the University of Missouri.

"College basketball is losing a great one," said Kansas coach Roy Williams. "I just can't picture Missouri basketball without Norm Stewart on the sideline."

Stewart's longevity at Missouri makes it difficult for any coach to imagine facing the Tigers in the Hearnes Center without "Stormin' Norman" prowling the sidelines.

"Norm Stewart is Missouri basketball," said Texas Christian coach Billy Tubbs, who had some

> "I always liked Norm," Tubbs said. "We had some battles on the court, but we always left it on the court."

classic battles with Stewart when he coached at Oklahoma.

"He's had as great a run as anybody can.

"You can't stay at a school for 32 years and not be someone special."

Tubbs, who verbally sparred with Stewart on many occasions as the Sooners coach, said their personal relationship was far different than their coaching relationship.

"I always liked Norm," Tubbs said. "We had some battles on the court, but we always left it on the court."

Of course, the two wouldn't be mistaken for best friends, either.

"Norm and I never grew up in this politically correct world," he said. "Now coaches hug after games. Norm and I never hugged. We were spit-in-your-eye-type guys."

Kansas State coach Tom Asbury shared a more

civil relationship with Stewart on, and off, the court.

Asbury was shocked by the announcement and disappointed to see Stewart leaving the coaching ranks.

"It's not always fun to play him, but he was fun to compete against," Asbury said.

That competitive fire was a trait every coach mentioned about Stewart.

Coach Stewart at his last Big 12 Tournament, March 12, 1999.
(Sean Meyers, Columbia Daily Tribune)

STEWART RETIRES

APRIL 1, 1999
Kent Heitholt

Even one of his bitterest foes was stunned and saddened by Norm Stewart's decision to step down as basketball coach at Missouri today.

Floyd Irons, the longtime head coach at Vashon High in St. Louis, has had more than a few disagreements with Stewart over the years. Today, he said there is no satisfaction in seeing the MU coach end his career.

"Norm and I were not the best of buddies over the years, but I respect what he's done. He did amazing things and he did it his way."

Former Kansas coach Ted Owens, now a vice president for Rebound Sports in Tampa, Florida, was one of Stewart's biggest rivals. Owens was the head man of the established team in the Big Eight when Stewart started to build a giant at MU.

"Even though Kansas and Missouri have been rivals since the Civil War, you still build up a respect for someone who did what he did," Owens said. "He came in when their program was not so good and built it into something. I have an admiration for what he did."

> "Even though Kansas and Missouri have been rivals since the Civil War, you still build up a respect for someone who did what he did," Owens said.

That's not to say Owens wasn't irked a time or two by Stewart.

"Of course," Owens said, "but he never bothered me as much as the Antlers."

Stewart built the program by landing some in-state recruits and lessening the talent pool for teams like Kansas, Kansas State and Oklahoma State. John Brown, an all-American at MU, was one of the first big-time recruits for the Tigers. With the addition of Al Eberhard, the Tigers became a force.

"He did more for us than just basketball, he taught us so much about life," Eberhard said. "I just know he's going to enjoy his retirement because he deserves it."

Eberhard suspects that Stewart's desire to keep Missouri competitive led to his decision.

"He had such an intense loyalty to the university and the state of Missouri, he never wanted to leave them without any players," Eberhard said.

Hickman coach Jim Sutherland, whose son Jason

was one of the Tigers' stars in recent seasons, said while Stewart's legacy is huge, there were tensions for players. Sutherland said his son's rough and tumble reputation around the Big Eight resulted from being asked to serve in that role for the team.

"Jason gained a lot from being at Missouri. In fact he signed with Missouri because of Norm Stewart," Sutherland said. "He was the kind of kid who would do whatever they asked.

"There's no doubt, it was tough on the kids to play at MU. But they got a lot out of it."

John Burns, a former Tiger captain who coaches high school basketball at Kearney, learned of Stewart's retirement on ESPN.

"I was shocked at first because I never expected it to happen this way," Burns said. "He was a very influential part of my life. He used to tell us that what happens to you isn't as important as how you react to it."

Today, everyone reacted in their own way.

Norm Stewart talks with the media at the press conference announcing his retirement. (Sean Meyers, Columbia Daily Tribune)

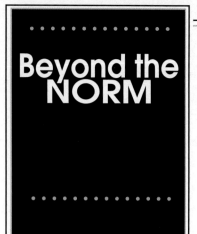

Beyond the NORM

HOMECOURT

APRIL 2, 1999
Ashley Williams

The regulars file in each morning at the little tavern on the town square, where an endless pot of coffee greets them each morning and conversation generally centers on crops and the weather.

But basketball still holds court in this small farm community, where Shelbyville's favorite native son made a name for himself long before he became synonymous with Tiger basketball.

Who could forget the state championship game against Center in December 1950? The score had been close all night. But with less than two minutes left, Shelbyville's blond, lanky guard stole the ball on an inbound pass and laid it in.

Leon Ralls was in the stands. "It happened so fast, the scorers didn't see it happen," Ralls said yesterday. "But the guy operating the clock, he got it right."

After a heated debate, the tournament ended in a tie and both teams were awarded first place.

The sign in front of the bandstand outside the Shelby County courthouse says it all: "Hometown of

> "It was great growing up there," Stewart said in an interview this morning. "I was the fourth child. I was the baby and had complete freedom. In those days there were no worries, you could run around the streets at night."

Norm Stewart."

Norman Stewart was born in 1935 in Leonard, an even smaller town 10 miles from Shelbyville in northeast Missouri.

He was too young for first grade, but because there wasn't anything better to do he followed his older siblings to school. Stewart remembers plopping himself down at a desk in Irene Rogers' class and how she didn't send him home.

The next school year, Stewart's family moved to what he describes as the "metropolitan" community of Shelbyville — population 756. His father owned the Standard Oil gas station, supplying fuel to farmers.

"It was great growing up there," Stewart said in an interview this morning. "I was the fourth child. I was the baby and had complete freedom. In those days there were no worries, you could run around the streets at night."

Summers were filled with swimming and baseball and visits to aunts, uncles and grandparents who lived nearby. The Capitol Cafe had an upstairs dance floor where kids congregated on Saturday nights to drink Cokes and dance.

"It was fun growing up in a small town," Stewart's sister, Jan Woods, recalled. "We just sort of lived in our own little hamlet."

Woods, who lives in Columbia, played basketball for the girls team.

"We went every place the boys did," she said. "We played the first game, and the boys played the second. Basketball was a big part of our lives."

Roy Blackford, who farms 1,200 acres in Shelby County, played with Stewart from 1949 to 1952.

"Of course, in the summertime we played baseball, but as soon as the weather started getting cool we played basketball," Blackford said. "We were fortunate then. We had an outstanding coach."

The coach's name was C. J. Kessler, and Stewart will never forget him.

"It would be like having Red Auerbach," the former Boston Celtics coach, "taking over a junior high team," Stewart said.

Ralls keeps a scrapbook at home filled with newspaper clippings and photographs of Shelbyville basketball. Some of his videotapes have the words "Norm Stewart" carefully printed in black ink on the label.

He remembers Stewart's prowess on the court. "He was a real good shot, he was a good ball handler and a team player. But I was most impressed with how smooth a ballplayer he was. He made it look easy."

Yesterday, Ralls and the rest of the gang at the Shelbyville Inn finished their coffee and headed home to tune in their televisions to watch Stewart, head coach at MU for 32 seasons, announce his resignation.

Rogers Hewitt, owner and publisher of the *Shelby County Herald* for 42 years, has followed Stewart's career. "He'll always be a local hero here, and people will welcome him back whether he's coaching basketball or if he isn't," Hewitt said. "The thing about Norm … is that he's never forgotten the people who were here when he grew up."

Donnie Ray worked for Stewart's father at Standard Oil and later bought the business. Ray used to take him to watch his son's home games in Columbia.

When the older Stewart passed away, Norm Stewart gave the Rays his dad's season tickets.

Ever since, Ray said, he and his wife have seldom missed a game.

Over the years, Stewart has returned to Shelbyville for the annual Old Settler's Reunion to catch up with friends and family.

"I'll go back and I might stand around the pool hall … and let's say we'd had an outstanding year, I might stand in the pool hall for five or 10 minutes before someone would say, 'Hey, Norm, are you still coaching down at Missouri?'"

Now that he's retired from coaching, Norm and his wife Virginia plan to share their new-found time with their grandchildren. (Photo courtesy of University of Missouri Sports Information)

Norm Stewart's 38-Year Coaching Career

Year	School	Record	Pct.	Conference
1961-62	Northern Iowa	19-5	.792	N/A
1962-63	Northern Iowa	15-8	.652	N/A
1963-64	Northern Iowa	23-4	.852	N/A
1964-65	Northern Iowa	16-7	.696	N/A
1965-66	Northern Iowa	13-7	.650	N/A
1966-67	Northern Iowa	11-11	.500	N/A
1967-68	Missouri	10-16	.385	5-9 (6)
1968-69	Missouri	14-11	.560	7-7 (5)
1969-70	Missouri	15-11	.577	7-7 (3t)
1970-71	Missouri	17-9	.654	9-5 (2t)
1971-72	Missouri	21-6	.778	10-4 (2)
1972-73	Missouri	21-6	.778	9-5 (2t)
1973-74	Missouri	12-14	.462	3-11 (7t)
1974-75	Missouri	18-9	.667	9-5 (3)
1975-76	Missouri	26-5	.839	12-2 (1)
1976-77	Missouri	21-8	.724	9-5 (2t)
1977-78	Missouri	14-16	.467	4-10 (6t)
1978-79	Missouri	13-15	.464	8-6 (2t)
1979-80	Missouri	25-6	.806	11-3 (1)
1980-81	Missouri	22-10	.688	10-4 (1)
1981-82	Missouri	27-4	.871	12-2 (1)
1982-83	Missouri	26-8	.765	12-2 (1)
1983-84	Missouri	16-14	.533	5-9 (6t)
1984-85	Missouri	18-14	.563	7-7 (3t)
1985-86	Missouri	21-14	.600	8-6 (3t)
1986-87	Missouri	24-10	.706	11-3 (1)
1987-88	Missouri	19-11	.633	7-7 (4)
1988-89	Missouri	29-8	.784	10-4 (2)
1989-90	Missouri	26-6	.813	12-2 (1)
1990-91	Missouri	20-10	.667	8-6 (4)
1991-92	Missouri	21-9	.700	8-6 (2t)
1992-93	Missouri	19-14	.576	5-9 (7)
1993-94	Missouri	28-4	.875	14-0 (1)
1994-95	Missouri	20-9	.690	8-6 (4)
1995-96	Missouri	18-15	.545	6-8 (6)
1996-97	Missouri	16-17	.485	5-11 (10)
1997-98	Missouri	17-15	.531	8-8 (5t)
1998-99	Missouri	20-9	.690	11-5 (4t)
Northern Iowa Totals		**97-42**	**.688**	**Six Years**
Missouri Totals		**634-333**	**.656**	**32 Years**
Career Totals		**731-375**	**.661**	**38 Years**

Winningest All-Time
Division I Coaches (By Wins)

Coach	Years	W
Dean Smith	36	879
Adolph Rupp	41	876
Henry Iba	41	767
Ed Diddle	42	759
Phog Allen	48	746
Bob Knight	33	742
NORM STEWART	**38**	**731**
Ray Meyer	42	724
Don Haskins	37	719
Lefty Driesell	36	711

Norm Stewart's Milestone Victories

CAREER

First	Northern Iowa 83, Macalester 57, 12/1/61
100th	MU 74, at Detroit 68, 12/16/67
200th	MU 73, Oklahoma 70 (at K.C.), 12/26/73
300th	MU 92, Oklahoma State 70, 2/27/79
400th	MU 69, Nebraska 63 (at K.C.), 3/11/83
500th	MU 91, North Carolina 81 (at New York), 11/23/89
600th	MU 99, UNC-Asheville 56, 1/3/93
700th	MU 75, Illinois 69 (at St. Louis), 12/23/97
731st	MU 54, at Texas 47, 2/27/99

MISSOURI

First	MU 74, at Arkansas 58, 12/2/67
100th	MU 68, UTEP 56, 12/8/73
200th	MU 67, at Kansas State 63, 2/21/79
300th	MU 84, Iowa State 66, 3/5/83
400th	MU 90, Iowa State 80 (at K.C.), 3/11/88
500th	MU 66, Illinois 65 (at St. Louis), 12/23/92
600th	MU 85, Oral Roberts 67, 12/10/97
634th	MU 54, at Texas 47, 2/27/99

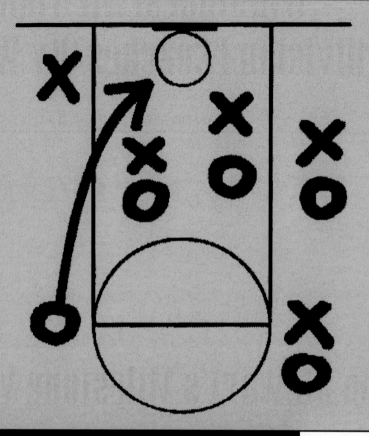

Congratulations to Norm Stewart on 32 great years at MU.

From your friends at State Farm Insurance!